Toyota's Global Marketing Strategy

Innovation through Breakthrough Thinking and Kaizen

Toyota's Global Marketing Strategy

Innovation through Breakthrough Thinking and Kaizen

Shozo Hibino
Koichiro Noguchi
Gerhard Plenert

CRC Press
Taylor & Francis Group
Boca Raton London New York

CRC Press is an imprint of the
Taylor & Francis Group, an **informa** business

A PRODUCTIVITY PRESS BOOK

CRC Press
Taylor & Francis Group
6000 Broken Sound Parkway NW, Suite 300
Boca Raton, FL 33487-2742

© 2018 by Shozo Hibino, Koichiro Noguchi, Gerhard Plenert
CRC Press is an imprint of Taylor & Francis Group, an Informa business

No claim to original U.S. Government works

Printed on acid-free paper

International Standard Book Number-13: 978-1-138-05941-2 (Hardback)

Library of Congress Cataloging-in-Publication Data

Names: Hibino, Shozo, 1940- author. | Noguchi, Koichiro, author. | Plenert, Gerhard Johannes, author.
Title: Toyota's global marketing strategy : innovation through breakthrough thinking and kaizen / Shozo Hibino, Koichiro Noguchi, Gerhard Plenert.
Description: Boca Raton, FL : CRC Press, [2017] | Includes bibliographical references.
Identifiers: LCCN 2017010294 | ISBN 9781138059412 (hardback : alk. paper)
Subjects: LCSH: Marketing--Planning. | Strategic planning. | Toyota Jidōsha Kabushiki Kaisha--Management.
Classification: LCC HF5415.13 .H48 2017 | DDC 658.8/02--dc23
LC record available at https://lccn.loc.gov/2017010294

Visit the Taylor & Francis Web site at
http://www.taylorandfrancis.com

and the CRC Press Web site at
http://www.crcpress.com

Contents

Preface

In his book *Management: Tasks, Responsibilities, Practices* (New York: Harper & Row), the late renowned business scholar Peter Drucker stated that conventional theories on marketing focus on merchandise sales. They say that marketing should be focused on selling more. Drucker argues that this is a sales theory, not a marketing theory. He emphasizes that marketing theory for both the present and the future should focus on the customer. We should seek a marketing theory that starts by recognizing what customers want and what value they receive, instead of what do we want to sell. We need to be asking what do our customers want to buy. Instead of advertising "what our products and services can do for you," we need to learn "what our customers value; what they need and want." Drucker asserted that a corporation has two fundamental customer-creating roles: marketing and innovation. He suggests that these two roles can be combined as one entrepreneurial role.

Toyota Motor Corp. is known for its practice of "Kaizen." But we need to ask a fundamental question: Was Toyota able to launch using only Kaizen? Kaizen is a necessary condition but not a sufficient one. This means that Toyota could not go global without Kaizen but that does not make it all encompassing. Drucker teaches that if there is no marketing integrated with innovation, you cannot be successful. For example, no matter how much we improve vinyl record marketing, it cannot ever beat the Internet music distribution business. Product improvement does not make sense unless it satisfies customer demand.

There have been numerous books published about Toyota that feature Kaizen as a way to improve manufacturing. This book takes us in a different direction. It is written by Koichiro Noguchi, who created Toyota's global marketing strategy, and by Shozo Hibino, who teaches innovative thinking practices and by Gerhard Plenert, former Director of Executive Education for the Shingo Institute, an institute focused on Enterprise Excellence. This book follows the previous thinking of Hibino's earlier book about Toyota's thinking habits, which initially highlighted global production. The current book focuses on Toyota marketing and how it ties back to Toyota's thinking habits.

Toyota is an amazing company with profits in excess of $20 billion per year. We have seen a deluge of books trying to explain why Toyota is so strong. However, being excellent does not imply long-lasting. It is estimated that of all the companies labeled as "excellent companies" in the book *In Search of Excellence*, less than 10% are still in existence. Demonstrating that there is a concern that Toyota may also suffer the same fate, we have recently seen the publication of books with titles like *Toyota Under Fire: Lessons for Turning Crisis into Opportunity*.

In Japan, and throughout the world, many large companies have declared bankruptcy. If Toyota stops following its historical thinking habits, the chances of Toyota facing a similar crisis increases. This book is an effort to preserve Toyota's thinking habits so that it can sustain its uniqueness by maintaining and sharing its historical practices with future generations. Readers, including Toyota officials, will benefit from the lessons taught in this book as they move forward globally.

Acknowledgments

The famous phrase "Standing on the shoulders of giants" is used in science. However, every contribution is equally important. Toyota's development and growth were accomplished by the effort of numerous great individuals. This book is the same, as many people have contributed to the writing of this book. This book's authors must thank each of them for their efforts.

First, the authors acknowledge Toyota's many great senior experts, published reference books, and the numerous papers listed in the end of this book. Each provided valuable content for this book.

Second, the authors thank the readers who have read the previous published books about Toyota's thinking habits and made helpful suggestions. This information was helpful in the creation of this book.

Third, this book was originally written in Japanese and was translated into English by Naoshi Miwa, who is a Certified Breakthrough Thinking Instructor and communications consultant.

Fourth, we received incalculable editorial assistance from Gerhard Plenert, who is the former director of Executive Education, Shingo Institute, Jon M. Huntsman School of Business, Utah State University; and coauthor with Shozo Hibino of the book *Making Innovation Happen: Concept Management through Integration.*

Fifth, we feel especially indebted to the editors, publishers, and agents involved in the distribution of this book and who worked with us toward this book's success.

Finally, we think that writing a book is for the benefit of our families as well as the reading public. We must acknowledge that the family suffers the most in the preparation of a book. Our deepest expression of appreciation for their patience and love during the trials involved in preparing this manuscript. This appreciation goes out to our wives, Shigemi, Harumi, and Renee. We dedicate the book to them and to our families.

The Japanese version of this book has the subtitle *Was Toyota Able to Launch Globally Using Only Kaizen?* The reader must now understand that the answer to this question is obviously no.

In conclusion, this book was created with the cooperation of numerous individuals. In addition to the original authors and the list of reference materials, numerous other people connected with Toyota shared their opinions and insight. The authors would like to express their gratitude to all these resources and for all of the support and advice given by those individuals and organizations who successfully practice Breakthrough Thinking in businesses, in the public sector, and even in farming.

Finally, this book benefitted from the work and personal assistance of Alexandria Gryder and Michael Sinocchi of Productivity Press. The authors would also like to acknowledge their persistent support.

Thank you.

Prologue

BLIND MEN DESCRIBING THE ELEPHANT

An ancient story tells of three blind men encountering an elephant. Since there was no elephant in their home country, they had no idea what an elephant was. They had no experience that would allow them to identify the elephant. Each of them touched the elephant in order to describe it. The blind man who touched its back leg claimed, "This animal like a tree," while another blind man touching its tail said, "This animal is slender like a snake because it is long and thin and wiggles around." The last blind man who was touching the elephant's trunk said, "No, you are both wrong. This animal is just like a person with delicate hands on the end of a sturdy arm."

This is a well-known story in the Jainist and Buddhist traditions. Toyota, like a big elephant, has been interpreted in various ways and many Toyota-related books have been published. They teach that Toyota is the Toyota Production System (TPS), or that Toyota is "Kaizen," or that Toyota is a "financial powerhouse," or that Toyota is "just-in-time," and so on. Many authors tried to characterize what Toyota stands for. None of them is wrong. All of the books describe characteristics of Toyota. When one of this book's authors, Shozo Hibino, previously published the book *Toyota Thinking Habits*, it created quite a stir, and it became a best seller. But in general, the reaction was that this was just one more piece of Toyota's Kaizen system.

This book deals with the Toyota elephant from a slightly different perspective. Previous Toyota-subject books were primarily written about production and gemba. Almost none dealt with marketing. The authors of this book explore Toyota's global marketing strategy using the lessons learned from previous books like *Toyota Thinking Habits, Making Innovation Happen*, and *Breakthrough Thinking*.

In their book *Profit Beyond Measure*, H. Thomas Johnson and Anders Broms (Japanese translation edition's title was Why Toyota Is Strong) the authors suggested that American managers working in Toyota's Georgetown, Kentucky, plant report that they are often asked questions by individuals who have just taken a tour of their plant. The guests would ask, "You showed us A, B, C, D, E, and even F. We have all of those items in our plants as well. If possible, would you show us G too?" Apparently they thought that Toyota had some type of special and secret weapon to differentiate itself from others. However, the employees would be forced to reply, "There is no special G. It doesn't exist."

Although this is an anecdote from Toyota's American experience, the same is true in Japan. There really is not much that is different at either Toyota. If one was to compare this story with the world of cooking, it would be easier to understand. When asked why food is delicious, they might answer that the food is not that different. The reason they can say this is because if there is a secret ingredient, it is cooked into the food at the time when the food was made. This "secret ingredient" can be hidden in such a way that others cannot easily imitate it. This book is about Toyota's secret ingredient. Rather than trying to identify Toyota's secret ingredient, which does not show up on any documents, the authors of this book suggest that you read about Toyota's "secret weapon," which will be described in this book.

Introducing the conclusion of this book first, we could refer to the "G" and say that this secret ingredient is the subject of this book. With regard to the question of why is Toyota strong, this book tries to find the answer using Toyota thinking habits, which were derived from new thinking paradigms called "Breakthrough Thinking" and "genetic thinking." These ideas have been inherited going back many generations to their roots at the time of Ieyasu Tokugawa, who unified a civil-war torn Japan in the seventeenth century. Particularly, this book points out that the strength of Toyota comes from its thinking habits and these are Toyota's secret ingredients.

The Toyota ingredients are, like in cooking, invisible and critical to the end result, but hard to find when you go on a plant tour. However, Toyota is not the only company using these ingredients. This book deals with the Toyota case, but there are companies with these excellent secret ingredients or thinking habits all around you. It would be valuable to identify those people or companies near you as you read through this book.

Like a coin, everything has two sides. We know some critics who assert that contractors of Toyota Motor have been subjugated by the company's policy of "don't let them live but don't let them die." However, this book looks at the positive side of Toyota and suggests we learn from Toyota's secret ingredients. Taking a positive perspective makes you feel courageous and hopeful. This book gives hope and energizes readers to find their own secret ingredients that will push them forward toward success.

We often claim that we cannot see what we look like. Your image in a mirror is a left-right reversed image and is not the true you. You can see yourself only when "looking at yourself from the outside." This book views Toyota from the inside using the perspective of Koichiro Noguchi and from the outside using the perspective of Shozo Hibino, who uses the lessons learned in the books *Toyota Thinking Habits and Breakthrough Thinking*. The authors wrote this book so that even those close to Toyota can nod their head in agreement with its message.

"LET'S OPEN THE DOOR. IT'S A BIG WORLD OUT THERE!!"

Sakichi Toyoda said to Kiichiro Toyoda, the founder of Toyota Motor, "Let's open the door. It's a big world out there!!"

Koichiro Noguchi, coauthor of this book, helped to write a book describing the history at Toyota. Noguchi started his career at Toyota after his university education and is a genuine Toyota-man equipped with all the Toyota thinking habits. In the spirit of Sakichi Toyoda's quote, Noguchi "opened windows to the world," when he went to graduate school in the United States as part of Toyota's overseas business staff where he learned a new way of thinking. He received specialized knowledge and earned an MBA, which broadened his expertise. He is a true implementer of global marketing at Toyota including hands-on experience with a joint venture with General Motors. He also has international procurement experience in a variety of different cultures, primarily in the United States where he held various posts such as sales planning and product planning.

Shozo Hibino is a seasoned business consultant for various clients including Toyota Motor and he has a vast amount of experience. His joint work with the late Gerald Nadler produced the book *Breakthrough Thinking*, which advocated moving away from old-fashioned reductionism thinking, which had existed since René Descartes. Hibino and Nadler's book has received worldwide attention.

Gerhard Plenert spent 12 years as a university faculty member, teaching at schools all over the world including Malaysia, England, and, of course, the United States. He has 20 years of consulting experience working for the largest as well as some of the smallest companies in the world. He has 19 published books (www.gerhardplenert.com).

Breakthrough Thinking calls for a new philosophy and approach to problem solving. It takes a 180-degree flip on traditional conventional thinking. Its impact on thinking focuses on the heliocentric theory advocated by Nicolaus Copernicus, who challenged people to use common sense about the earth-centered theory. Just as René Descartes and his followers advocated a switchover from divine thinking to reductionist thinking, Nadler and Hibino have advocated that mankind should make another switch to a new kind of thinking. In our contemporary way of thinking, the solution of one problem often generates another problem, similar to the whack-a-mole arcade game. Problems are growing in number at a geometric rate, making people feel like they are pounding their heads against brick walls. Descartes's world in the sixteenth century called for a thinking transformation since the current divine thinking approach brought only confusion. Similarly, in our world today, with its growing list of contradictions and the resulting confusion in our daily lives, mankind has come to a stage where another thinking transformation is needed.

In this book, the reader will first learn the meaning of Toyota thinking habits at the beginning of the book. Then the reader will discover a resonance between an actioner and a theorist in the following chapters.

Toyota Motor has an entrepreneurial spirit born in a mountain village in Japan in the old Mikawa region (Aichi, today). As Toyota opened its windows, it became one of the largest corporations in the world. The authors hope that the readers also receive a drive for "higher aspirations" from this book and will boldly strive to go beyond boundaries into the wider world. The authors suggest that we "open windows. Outer space is even wider." We need to "boldly go where no man has gone before!" (*Star Trek*).

1

Introduction: What Does Toyota's "Thinking Habits" Mean? What Is the Toyota Way of Thinking?

THINKING NEEDS TO BECOME A HABIT

It is said a man makes decisions 50,000 times a day. For example, when waking up we face the decisions of should I get up now, should I wash my face, should I brush my teeth, and so on. Consciously or subconsciously our daily life is full of decisions that affect our behavior. This series of decisions has become habitual as part of our daily routine. A lazy life without any exercise eventually leads to a disastrous lifestyle inevitably filled with sickness and disease. Eventually it may potentially cause our death. This book raises our awareness that the same thing could happen to your "thinking habits." It advocates an improved thinking process using as an example the thinking processes of people at the Toyota Motor Company.

By repeating the 50,000 decisions daily we would, after a couple years, achieve a set of results. Some results may be random and accomplish some good results, while others fail. This concept also fits a business corporation. By maintaining poor thinking habits, a company would soon find itself with a corporate thinking habit disease, which may result in its bankruptcy. The root strength of Toyota lies in its thinking habits.

We are all under the influence of our historical and social environment, which defines our thinking and our behavior. Through long years, habits, and tradition have been influencing our decision making and bringing about various consequences. It is also true that decision making is a habit that differs by region, culture, race, and religion. For example, the thinking habits of the Muslims have been defined by their god Allah. Similarly, Jewish thinking habits and Japanese thinking habits are different from each other. Shozo Hibino, one of the authors of this book, has been engaged in an international joint study using several international cooperation programs. Over the years, he encountered different thinking habits and often felt puzzled. When studying in the United States he met a roommate, a young Jewish man from Brooklyn, New York. The Jewish people did not expect any protection from any nation when they had no home country. This roommate insisted that either money and/or knowledge is what they cherish and the author was puzzled. But it turned out that this gave Hibino the opportunity to learn Jewish thinking habits. Thanks to this experience Hibino was able to have better human relations with the Jewish community in the following years and he found that the majority of his research collaborators were Jewish. For example, *Breakthrough Thinking*, which is one of the backbones of this book, was coauthored by Hibino and the late Gerald Nadler, professor emeritus at the University of Southern California, who was Jewish.

Racial conflicts can be attributed to the different thinking habits of different cultures. Thus, thinking habits, which are greatly influenced by geography, history, culture, religion, or customs, are identified as a prime driver of behavior in our world. This book, however, focuses on thinking habits from the perspective of a thinking paradigm theory rather than from the perspective of culture, religion, or geography.

Around the world, we see situations where people from particular regions are outstanding and successful at business. Needless to say, the Jewish community fits that description. Additionally, many Chinese people coming from the province of Fujian fit this description. This would include many successful Indians coming from a region in India called Marwar. Why did these people successfully make fortunes all over the world? This book hints at answers to this question. These cultures are driven by their thinking habits. We find the same in Japan where they praise traditionally successful Ohmi merchants that come from today's Shiga Prefecture. They are extremely effective at selling, buying, and socializing. More currently in Japan we hear expressions such as the "Hitachi people," who are a group of more independent-minded samurai/warriors, or "Mitsubishi people," who behave like feudal lords. These terms are used to describe the thinking habits of these individuals.

THE SIX THINKING HABITS OF THE MIKAWA SAMURAI

Toyota Motor was born in a part of Aichi Prefecture called Mikawa, which is also the birthplace of the Tokugawa family that governed Japan for 267 years (1600–1867) and drove its expansion into the world. Interestingly, Mikawa and its neighboring region called Enshu sprouted similar companies that went global such as Honda, Suzuki, Yamaha, and Kawai. Why did this particular region create global corporation giants? Is there a hidden secret in the thinking habits of the Mikawa region that is similar to that of the Jewish merchants, overseas Chinese, or Indian tradesmen? This book explores answers for this question by first comparing the thinking habits of Ieyasu Tokugawa, the founder of the 267-year-long Tokugawa Shogunate, and his loyal subordinates belonging to the Samurai class, against Toyota Motor who we see today as a global automotive manufacturing giant.

Tokugawa and his samurai from Mikawa had common thinking habits that respected such values as

Simplicity/fortitude
Frugality/efforts
Honest poverty/wealth building
Austerity
Long-term perspective/long-range planning
Peace and prosperity within one's family

A neighbor of this Mikawa region is a region called Owari. These two regions have merged into what is now called Aichi Prefecture. It is here that two historically impressive individuals were born during the civil-war days of Japan: Nobunaga Oda and Hideyoshi Toyotomi. The differences between Oda and Tokugawa are often attributed to the differences between the traditional regions of Owari and Mikawa. Like Oda, a legendary razzmatazz hero, Owari often focused on showing off his flashiness. Mikawa is a less spectacular place. Toyota Motor seems to have inherited the thinking genes of Mikawa and Owari. For example, the robustness of Nagoya's economy today and how it was seemingly immune from the crazy economic bubbles in the 1990s is believed to be deeply rooted in the thinking habits of its own region. Those thinking habits, the authors believe, are not stylish and savvy. On the contrary, this region has been praised by the rest of the country with statements like "Nagoya is a great countryside city" or "Toyota is just like a provincial lord."

Let's consider Toyota from the perspective of the six thinking habits of Mikawa samurai/warriors.

1. Simplicity/fortitude—Similar to the ruggedness of the old Mikawa samurai, we often witness a similar dedication to work in the employees of Toyota throughout the production facilities in the Toyota assembly lines. We see it in the Denso factory, in the Aisin Seiki facility, and in the offices of Toyota's auto parts sales departments. Overseas trainees to Japan, who the authors often trained, were deeply impressed with Toyota employees who worked silently and with dedication just like the old samurai. The author Hibino often receives comments from others who work with Toyota that its employees are all quietly hard working without the need to be flamboyant.

2. Frugality/efforts—Frugality and efforts are often talked about in conjunction with simplicity and fortitude. For this value we see the influence of the thinking habits taken from Ho-Toku-Kyo (a form of Eastern philosophy), which was advocated by Sontoku Ninomiya and was widespread in the communities of the Mikawa region. Ninomiya advanced values like sincerity, sensibleness, small efforts accumulate to become a large harvest, diligence, compromise, and teamwork. Simply put, he tried to motivate people to work hard and live by principles, such as living within their income, building on small efforts, saving money, gaining power by setting a common goal, and ultimately contributing to the community and the nation-at-large. The Mikawa samurai succeeded using this same ideology.

These same teachings influenced Toyota's thinking habits. In Massaaki Sato's book *The House of Toyota*, he stated that "as he graduated from the First High School, he chose to attend Nagoya University rather than the University of Tokyo because that was where Kiichiro (Toyoda) and Eiji (Toyoda) studied." Kiichiro wanted his son Shoichiro, the heir apparent of the Toyoda family, to get familiar with the Mikawa culture. Kiichiro feared his son would never get a chance to inherit the Toyota spirit (their thinking habits), which incorporated simplicity/fortitude and frugality/diligent effort, unless his son spent time in the home of Toyota during his most informative years. The authors wonder if Kiichiro Toyoda, as the son of the founder of the business Sakichi, had challenges inheriting the conventional thinking habits of the Mikawa and whether that was part of reason behind introducing him in their culture.

3. Honest poverty/wealth building: An alliance of Toyota is Toyota Bank, which reinforces its policy of nonborrowing. This reinforces and demonstrates Toyota's thinking habits of honest poverty/wealth building. Unlike many corporations that fell to the temptation of increasing debt during the economic bubble, Toyota never stopped building its own personal wealth during those years. Its performance was impressive. It is not uncommon to hear news reports saying "having recorded over $14 billion in profit, Toyota ought to loosen its wallet a bit." Following the Mikawa thinking habits, Toyota ignores such comments. Sakichi Toyoda is quoted as saying, "It is more difficult to spend than to earn money." The wallet of Toyota is not easily loosened. Toyota is known for its meticulous effort to remove waste in all areas of its operations, including controlling the practice of spending money, a process that it optimizes. The practice of removing any wasteful spending is accepted by all as a matter-of-fact at Toyota.

   This practice is not confined by looking only at Mikawa traditions, but it is a practice found all around the central part of Japan including the old Owari, Mino, and Ise areas. Take for example Nagoya, the biggest city in the region, where a standard noodle can only be sold after adding a bowl of rice, or housewives only go shopping after having checked all advertising flyers and then choosing to shop around, going out of their way to buy the same item at a different location even if it is just a yen cheaper. This practice is very common for this region.

4. Austerity—Austerity can be demonstrated using a peculiar thinking habit that is often explained by the expression of "attempting to squeeze a drop of water out of a dried dust cloth." Clearly, this is a thinking habit that is inherited over generations in the Mikawa region long after Ieyasu Tokugawa. At Toyota this behavior is exemplified in their pursuit of the three "Mu's" of Mura (unevenness), Muri (irrationalness), and Muda (wastefulness). These Mu's manifest in the austerity thinking habit. The Toyota mission statement, compiled by Kiichiro Toyoda, stresses that we "should be cautious about

joviality but rather stay simple and fortitudinous." This embodies Toyota's values as well as its thinking habits. No matter how often people say Toyota is unrefined, Toyota sticks to the belief that "the only one who guards our castle is us." The statement exemplifies the strength of Toyota. As we see more of the castles of big corporations falling, both in the past and in the present, we become more convinced of the significance and validity of the thinking habits of Toyota.

There is one more point we should stress. It is extremely difficult to negotiate business transactions in this region. This challenge is not confined to Toyota. Contracts become valid only after thorough cost evaluations. They often use what is referred to as "three cuts" before the completion of any business transaction. They are (1) initial discount negotiations occur at the first meeting followed by, (2) the second discount request at the signing of a contract, and then (3) another 10% price slashing at the time of payment using the pressure of future business relations claiming that the payer retains the amount in their own account dependent on future performance. Unless you are aware of this business practice, your business could encounter a large loss. As a result, in Mexico and China they have the habit of doing business starting with significantly inflated prices. Clearly we need to be familiar with their thinking habits in order to effectively do business with these organizations. As the saying goes, "When in Rome, do as the Romans do!"

5. Long-term perspective/long-range planning—Toyota inherits the thinking gene of Ieyasu Tokugawa, who conquered Japan using strategy and tactics. When the American automobile industry was in deep trouble, Eiji Toyoda, former president of Toyota, chose a strategy to help a rival producer by advocating "competition and concord." They signed a joint venture contract with General Motors that led to the startup New United Motor Manufacturing Incorporated (NUMMI) (Figure 1.1). Tatsuro Toyoda, former managing director of Toyota Motor, was the first president of this newborn joint-venture company. Toyota expected to learn GM's production process and sales experience in the U.S. marketplace, and GM was anxious to learn the Toyota Production System, which included its Lean production techniques. NUMMI was later dissolved as the joint-venture contract expired. Now Toyota runs its own assembly plants in the

FIGURE 1.1
Signing of joint venture business with GM. (From "Toyota 75 Years History.")

United States, and GM seems to have reverted to its old traditional ways of operation.

As for the Chinese market, Toyota is often said to be a late entrant. But this delay is often attributed to its inherent thinking habits focused on long-term perspective/long-range planning. When Ieyasu Tokugawa was weak, he joined with his rival Hideyoshi Toyotomi and they became an integrated army. We now ask if it was a smart move for Toyota to team up with GM when the latter was in a weak position. It appears to have been a good move for Toyota.

6. Peace and prosperity within one's family—Finally, it is safety within the family that is cherished both within Toyota and with the Mikawa samurai. Toyota's management places the safety of the Toyota Group as its core value. They boast about their ability to maintain consistent, steady employment, and to take care of their employees. Within the principles of Toyoda we find the spiritual backbone of all Toyota corporate families. This includes the statement that "we should show compassion, show fraternity, and encourage good relationships within the family." It is generally agreed that these thinking habits have been functioning and are key elements in building Toyota

personnel and in creating a family of all Toyota group corporations. Hibino, this book's author, once had his laboratory in Toyota City. This location is filled with areas where Toyota employees gather to enjoy each other's company in a family-like atmosphere. Although Toyota learned a lot from its joint venture in the United States, Toyota insisted on incorporating Kiichiro's belief that "labor is our most important asset and is not a cost." Moody's had devalued its assessment of Toyota because it maintains a practice of lifelong employment. They considered this as a negative business practice. However, Toyota had a strong response against this perspective. Toyota values human resources as a treasure and considers it nonsense for foreign institutions like Moody's to criticize Toyota's thinking habits, which Toyota considers a source of its strength. Toyota resents other cultures that consider humans as a cost of doing business. It is difficult to change Moody's assessment, but this is fundamentally something that needs to be changed in the American perspective or thinking habits.

The six thinking habits that we have discussed are critical thinking habits, and unfortunately it often seems that only those who are directly involved with Toyota and its affiliates can comprehend their true value. Ex-president Eiji Toyoda once boasted that "Toyota is said to be Kintaro-ame" (this is a stick candy bar with the pattern of the face of Kintaro, a cheerful boy hero; the face appears when the candy bar is sliced). What he was saying was that all Toyota people, either from Denso or Aisin Seiki or wherever, share the same thinking habits. In other words, all people belonging to the larger Toyota group (the extended Toyota supply chain) maintain the identical thinking habits inherited from the Tokugawa era. It is important to note that Toyota and its Toyota network are not a Kintaro candy. All factories and affiliates are different. But at a higher level when we look at the thinking habits of this network of organizations, Eiji's words take on significance and meaning.

In this analysis of Toyota from the perspective of thinking habits, the reader can understand that Toyota has inherited a very unique thinking gene or structure. This book's author Noguchi is just one of the many individuals in this Toyota network to have inherited this same thinking gene, and using this he was able to develop the habits that have opened global windows.

WHO ESTABLISHED TOYOTA'S THINKING HABITS?

Toyota's thinking habits were inherited from the thinking genes of the Mikawa samurai as taught by Ieyasu Tokugawa. After their establishment, these "thinking habits" acquired a large following. This book highlights and focuses on following four individuals who are primarily responsible for the creation of the Toyota thinking habits:

Sakichi Toyoda
Kiichiro Toyoda (the founder of Toyota Motor)
Taizo Ishida (influential contributor in the development of Toyota Motor)
Taiichi Ohno (originated the Toyota Production System)

In this book we will review how Toyota's thinking habits evolved over many years. It is important to note that these four individuals are all descendants of the Japanese Mikawa and Owari samurai class.

Sakichi Toyoda was born in a poor mountain village west of Lake Hamana (presently the city of Kosai). He inherited the thinking habits of the Mikawa samurai believing in the principles of hard work, saving, and humble living. He invented a revolutionary loom machine and made his fortune with it, but he maintained his humble lifestyle. His enormous savings became the capital that allowed the family to later move into the automobile business. The traditional Mikawa country had a widespread belief that "good work should be rewarded" from the teachings of Sontoku Ninomiya and the Nichiren Buddhism sect. They strongly influenced Sakichi's thinking habits. His son Kiichiro and the group he organized created the principles later followed by Toyota. We can now see where Sakichi's thinking habits were beautifully incorporated. These thinking habits include:

1. Senior and junior individuals alike should devote themselves to the service and productivity of the country's industrial sector.
2. Focus on the mind. Studying and invention should be the focus. Look ahead for contemporary trends.
3. Admonish luxury but stay humble and Spartan.
4. Focus on family unity and friendship. Encourage a strong family atmosphere.
5. Respect religious values and live every day with gratitude and thankfulness.

These five Toyoda principles became a foundation of future credos and mission statements for many companies, including Toyota Motor, Toyota Industries, Denso, Toyota Auto Body, and Aisin Seiki, where the thinking habits of the old Sakichi still live on. The authors believe that even after the globalization of Toyota, the original Toyoda principles were revised, but the underlying thinking habits and spirit remain are unchanged. Changing these would mark the beginning of the end of Toyota. The vitality of this and any other corporation is defined by its thinking habits. For the continued progress of Toyota, it needs to sustain and improve while maintaining a focus on the Toyota thinking habits.

Sakichi Toyoda's son, Kiichiro Toyoda, was also born in an old Yamaguchi Village in Yoshida Country in Mikawa. He is also a genuine Mikawa guy. He was strongly influenced by his father when he ventured into the automobile business, which was considered to be a reckless venture in those days.

Sakichi's development overlaps with the life of Ieyasu Tokugawa, who had just started a small competitive feud in Mikawa. His goal was to grow and surpass his larger counterparts and finally attain the position of the conqueror of Japan. This drove Kiichiro to the brink of bankruptcy in 1949 because of the financial crunch caused by the Dodge product line and a financial tightened policy in Japan during the occupation after World War II. Bank consortiums demanded he restructure the employees in the company, which meant a layoff, in exchange for the financing that he needed causing him to leave Toyota in frustration.

The successor to Kiichiro was Taizo Ishida from the old Owari country, present-day Tokoname Aichi, who is remembered as the person who rejuvenated Toyota. Ishida was personally trained by Sakichi Toyoda and was called the "great headmaster." His favorite phrase was "Defend your own castle by yourself." With this phrase he was proudly asserting "what was wrong with the country spirit." He was talking about Kiichiro, who saw trouble in Toyota's financing and was finally forced to resign. Ishida insisted, "don't do anything wasteful" and "always ensure your ultimate savings." He embedded these thinking habits into Toyota. He lived in his cozy residence close to this book's author Hibino, who still enjoys contact with Ishida's grandson. Hibino remembers the family as being very humble and living simply.

The next person who had a strong influence on and who contributed to the strengthening of the Toyota thinking habits of Mikawa and Owari as they are now embedded into Toyota, and who should be unforgettable, is Taiichi Ohno. Ohno was born in today's Kariya, Aichi, and was an offspring of a genuine Mikawa samurai. His ancestry traces back to Toshikatsu Doi, a chief minister during the Edo years. He was born to a good family and his father served as both the mayor of Kariya and as a member of the House of Representatives. Ohno graduated from what is known today as the Nagoya Institute of Technology. Ohno got a job at Toyota Boshoku, a textile company, where he worked hard with Kiichiro to build the foundation of today's Toyota. The culture of the Kariya region is characterized as a spirit of defiance. This "defiance" became instilled into Toyota's thinking habits by Ohno. His greatest contribution was his creation of the Toyota Production System known for its practice of just-in-time and the kanban systems. Needless to say, over the years this production methodology has been a major contributor to Toyota's growth.

There are many other people who inherited and influenced Toyota's thinking habits, such as Eiji Toyoda, who built on the thinking habits of Sakichi and Kiichiro Toyoda in support of Toyota's growth. He, too, inherited the thinking habits of old Mikawa samurai. Another is Shotaro Kamiya, known as a god of car sales, who was born in old Owari, currently Chita country, Aichi. He is a great contributor for installing the nation-wide sales network for Toyota cars all over Japan. Then there is Masaya Hanai, who considered himself a pupil of Taizo Ishida and admired Ieyasu Tokugawa. He asserted his belief in stinginess with a focus on saving money in order to build a solid foundation for the "Bank of Toyota." He was from Otowa, Aichi, another Mikawa township, with the reputation as a humble individual with Spartan values.

ENACTING "THE TOYOTA WAY" IN 2001

Starting from a mountain village in old Mikawa, Toyota evolved into a global entity with a large number of employees. When it was still a small company in Mikawa, it was easy to share cultural values without explicitly stating them in words. However, since the 1970s, as Toyota's operations became international, it saw behavior fragmentation in its diversified culture and in the values of the employees in different locations. This created a need to compile what had previously been implicit in the knowledge and ideas of Toyota's thinking habits, as nurtured by Sakichi and Kiichiro Toyada. They needed to explicitly state Toyota's values and methods so they could be shared and standardized across the entire global workforce. A document describing Toyota's values was created and called "The Toyota Way 2001." It specifies the Toyota corporate vision and mission showing the culture that should exist within the company. It was shared with all Toyota employees all over the world.

The two pillars of The Toyota Way 2001 are

1. Wisdom and Kaizen
2. Respect of humanity

The earlier focus in some areas of the organization on the constant pursuit of higher values by exploiting human wisdom was not satisfied in the new pillars. For example, "respect of humanity" focuses on individual development and growing it toward successful corporate achievement by respecting all stakeholders. Figure 1.2 is the conceptual framework of "The Toyota Way 2001," where you can see the business philosophy of Toyota wherein they grow human capability while respecting humanity.

In marketing, the original model of "The Toyota Way 2001" can be found in the efforts of Shotaro Kamiya, who was responsible for all of Toyota's sales and marketing efforts. Kamiya emphasized and focused on "respecting car dealers." He identified powerful stakeholders in each region and

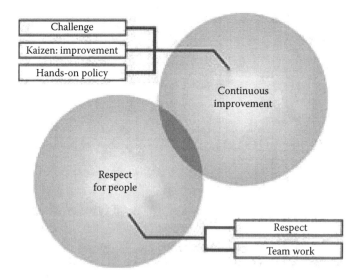

FIGURE 1.2
"The Toyota Way 2001." (From Toyota website. http://www.toyota-global.com/company /history-of-toyota/75years/data/conditions/philosophy/toyotaway2001.html.)

used them to build a nationwide network of dealerships. This same idea was later applied in the United States, where Toyota developed an afford-able and efficient network of dealers.

At this point the authors would like to cite the actual comments of Fujio Cho, president when "The Toyota Way 2001" was released:

> Since its very foundation, Toyota has put into practice its belief in a need to contribute the pursuit of better manufacturing processes to society. In its quest toward this goal Toyota created a unique management system of beliefs and values. This includes the development of new methods of man-agement and new tools for job execution. All these have become the source of Toyota's competitiveness. However, not all of these beliefs and values were clearly stated or clearly defined. What we considered to be common-sense methods and which should naturally be employed are not necessar-ily generally understood. These beliefs, values, and methods, shared now implicitly, must be sustained and inherited, and continue to evolve as prime contributors for the growth of a global Toyota. Particularly, as our business is expanding, our business domains are also expanding. We are now working with people who have different values and it is essential for us to share our management convictions and values to secure our identity as a global Toyota entity.
>
> At this time, we found it necessary to organize and summarize those management philosophies and values which are inherent inside Toyota and which have been "implicit knowledge" and document them explicitly in a document called "The Toyota Way 2001" so everyone can comprehend and understand them. Our primary focus in doing this is for unity amongst all of us working at Toyota. I am convinced that "The Toyota Way 2001" should be supported and followed by additional creative management ideas and methods which will continue to define explicitly each job function allowing The Toyota Way to be expanded even further.
>
> The Toyota Way should evolve but also remain the foundational source of strength of Toyota. I would like everyone to search for opportunities sup-porting their thinking from now on with a focus on the question, "Is it a Toyota way?" while further applying this thinking to each of your specific job environments. What would be The Toyota Way in your case? How should it be reflected in or applied to your job? How should it influence behavior in the future? We need each of you to aggressively join in this discussion. This chain of thinking would ensure the growth, recognition, and sharing of The Toyota Way, allowing it to go through its own evolution and growth.

Cho's address shows that The Toyota Way is not fixed and that it needs to keep evolving. Over time there were many new ideas that were added to

The Toyota Way such as Kaizen or the "enhancement of 'diamond innovation' in all aspects," which this book explains and emphasizes in more detail in the following chapters.

It is the authors' hope that the reader understands that the Toyota thinking habits are the result of inheriting the thinking gene of the old Mikawa-Owari region, which has existed from ancient times until the present time.

This section gave us a brief glimpse into Toyota's thinking habits and why it is a key perspective for this book. In the next chapter, we will focus on "Breakthrough Thinking," another key concept discussed in this book, that Toyota introduced in its "Work Design" in 1963, which was the forerunner of the current concept of Breakthrough Thinking and is deployed in various parts in the company. It is important to understand the connection between Toyota's thinking habits and how they relate to the concept of Breakthrough Thinking or Work Design, which this book explains in future chapters.

Question for Reflection

Discuss how thinking habits influence marketing strategies.

2

Secret Ingredient #1: Don't Chase Tradition—The Uniqueness Principle

START FROM THE "NOTHING-NOTHING SYNDROME"

The Toyota Motor Corp. started with Kiichiro Toyoda, son of Sakichi Toyoda, during a trip to Europe. He felt that the age of cars was around the corner. But Toyota's startup years were filled with fierce struggles. There were no technology, no parts, and no materials. He had to come from a state of having nothing. He initially attempted to manufacture a car using the example of an existing automobile. But he kept being turned down. For example, a major steel producer was uninterested in supplying steel sheets for a tiny company like Kiichiro's workshop. There was no way to procure steel for his car. Kiichiro decided that it would be better to produce his own steel so he bought his own furnace. Similarly, he acquired other elements of the vehicle. He acquired casting expertise and forming equipment for shaping the car. His original tiny iron workshop became today's Aichi Steel, a Toyota group company, specializing in the manufacture of forged steel products such as crankshafts and gears.

Shozo Hibino, one of this book's authors, has been engaged in the training of people from developing countries for over four decades. Many of them told him, lamenting their shortage for resources, that they needed Toyota to help them or they would not be able to succeed because of these shortages. This phenomenon is called the "nothing-nothing syndrome" and it is a thinking habit focused on deficiencies. On the contrary, what they need are healthy thinking habits that will enable them to deal with the situations like having nothing available by drawing wisdom from a more positive thinking habit. They should learn from Kiichiro and see how he overcame the nothing-nothing syndrome during his early years.

Kiichiro, who inherited the thinking habits of his father Sakichi, and who was strengthened by his belief in his creative and independent abilities and in his self-reliance, boldly challenged the advanced Western automobile manufacturers. He not only transferred technologies from those countries, he dared to engage himself in the challenging battle of entering into the automobile industry using indigenous technology. His thinking habit has been incorporated into today's Toyota, as can be seen in its credo "always focus attention to research and development in order to stay ahead." We can see that this is accurate when we recognize the world-renowned innovations like the Toyota Production System (TPS), hybrid cars such as the Prius, and the futuristic Mirai, a hydrogen fuel cell car. These are the results of thinking habits focused on pursuing the exploration of new ideas and new product development.

WHAT DOES IT MEAN TO PURSUE UNIQUENESS?

Today we can learn a lot from the thinking habits of historical heroes such as Nobunaga Oda or Iyeyasu Tokugawa, as well as the unique and passionate thinking habits of Kiichiro Toyoda. Here are some examples:

1. There is a thinking habit that focuses attention on the principle that "everything is the same." Kiichiro did not adopt this perspective. He rejected the idea of employing the same methods of production when trying to make the same kinds of automobiles. Instead he felt he had to figure out a different production method on his own because Japan is different from Western countries. As a result, Toyota came up with the concept of just-in-time (JIT). People from all over the world are now attracted to tours of advanced examples of JIT as they seek to copy this methodology.

   a. The issues that Ford faces today are similar to Toyota in the past. Ford should be introduced to Toyota's methodologies. Unfortunately, following the "everything is the same" thinking habit drives people into a kind of mental stagnation or a thinking habit focused on a "dependence upon precedents" (dependence on what others are doing and on what has come before). Following Kiichiro's thought process and realizing that Japan and the West are different, it is critical for everyone to do their own creative thinking and develop something specific to them, thereby winning their own creativity battles.

2. Toyota has become an expert at creating "systems." Similar to how the Oda–Tokugawa coalition army won its war using its system that incorporated a three-stage process for firing rifles, Toyota also created its own system of a "Just-in-Time Toyota Production System," thereby challenging the automotive market and charging boldly into the world marketplace. A critical point is that we must incorporate new thinking habits where we use systems such as the three-stage rifle shooting process rather than using a single rifle unit. This three-stage rifle shooting process effectively works the same as the modern machine gun, setting up a barrage of rapid fire in front of the enemy (we will return to a discussion of this shooting system in future chapters).

3. It is critical to make changes using a methodology of process improvement rather than simply driving results. Using Kaizen projects focused on continuous process improvements will result in higher-quality products and consequently have a more significant product impact. It is essential to stress that quality should be built into every process.
   a. Merit-based pay systems that pay employees based on the number of units produced or using final inspections rather than in-line inspections are popular in many companies. However, Toyota's thinking habit would reject this system. To Toyota it sounds like nonsense.

4. Customers see themselves as having a distinctive uniqueness. They are telling Toyota about the need for a thinking habit that gives us the flexibility to occasionally adjust ourselves to our uniqueness.

5. Independent product and process development is rooted in Toyota's thinking habits and Toyota rejects any imitation. Toyota prefers to think through issues on its own.

These five thinking habit examples exemplify the teachings of Sakichi and Kiichiro Toyoda. A thinking habit focused on pursuing uniqueness has taken root in Toyota. Words and phrases have been invented by Toyota that are now part of the business lexicon. Examples would include:

Just-in-time
Genryu-kanri (control at a source)
Shitsuke (compliance to rules, well trained)
Single-minute dandori (setting up of dies and tools)

Andon (process flow lights displayed in the factory)
Gemba principle (hands-on "go and observe" approach)
Kanban, Shikumi, Heijunka (leveled production)
Poka-yoke (fail safe)

These Japanese terms are the result of successfully integrating the thinking habits of Sakichi and Kiichiro, who created and sent these new concepts out into the world.

THE THINKING HABITS TOYOTA REJECTED

When Toyota was still a long way from becoming a global player, the company imported machine tools from then–West Germany. A year passed and the president of the German tool manufacturer visited a Toyota factory. The German president expected to see his products in use throughout the facility. He tried in vain to find his company's products. Wondering why, he asked an executive of Toyota, "Did you sell off our machine tools? I could not find any." The answer was "No, Mr. president. The production line itself was made by your machine tools." Toyota took a full year to improve the German machine tools and convert them into Toyota-made machine tools. Surprised with the production innovation, the German president reportedly started evaluating Toyota's technical expertise to see how he could incorporate some of its own products and innovations.

This event took place long ago, but it exemplifies another side of Toyota's thinking habits, which is to try to "Toyota-ize" anything learned from the outside and attempt to fit it within Toyota's unique culture, rather than adopting it as is. When Work Design was introduced to Toyota, Toyota-ization took place. Hibino, the book's author, taught Breakthrough Thinking at many of Toyota affiliates. Different from most traditional companies, the author found Toyota's training coordinator busy taking notes during the training session. He was in the process of Toyota-izing the training content. After a couple of years, the ideas from the course were adopted into the organization as a newly developed "Toyota way of training" and consequently became part of the thinking habits of Toyota.

Catalog engineering occurs when companies build their assembly lines using the catalogs of industrial machinery makers. This is how most companies assemble their lines. Engineers who practice this thinking habit are referred to as catalog engineers. However, at Toyota, an engineer's job is not finished unless he incorporates wisdom after the trial runs of the newly purchased equipment in order to Toyota-ize its operation. Most automation machinery is fast and continuously running. However, they are modified to stop operations automatically when a defect is produced (self-evaluation), giving the Toyota process an edge up over competitors. Its thinking habit to constantly pursue uniqueness has become Toyota's overwhelming strength.

OPENING THE AMERICAN MARKET

Japan was destined to grow its economy using trade since it was lacking in natural resources. It uses the importing and processing of huge volumes of resources and converts them into products that are the sold in the global marketplace. This is how Japan supports its more than 120 million people. In the post–WWII years, Japan has effectively played the role in the world factory thanks to its workaholic employees. Once called "cheap but poor in quality" or "Japanese junk," the Japanese products have been substantially refined and improved over the years, as can be seen in industry sectors like home electronics and semiconductors. This is attributable to the attention given to meticulous detail, resulting in the growing popularity of Japanese products in the world marketplace. However, the stronger competitiveness of "Made in Japan" products triggered trade friction in various locations, particularly in the United States, as demonstrated in the case of the textile trade in the late 1960s, steel products and electronics in the late 1970s, cars and semiconductors in the 1980s, and high-tech engineering in the 1990s.

Ex-President Eiji Toyoda mentioned in his book *Ketsudan* [Decision Making] that "in reference to the Japan–US trade friction after the second oil crisis, as far as the automobile is concerned, the friction did not occur because of the difference of the strength of the car assemblers in the two countries. The increased export of Japanese-made cars to the United States was the result of the smart management by Japanese car assemblers after the two oil crises. The oil crises were bad luck for American car makers. To put it other way, the Japanese counterparts were blessed with good luck. It is quite natural that American automotive manufacturers would feel frustrated since Japanese assemblers were smarter in handling the situation." We saw Americans discrediting Japanese cars in various parts of the United States. American labor also showed its strong opposition to Japanese automobiles. It was in this environment that the book's author Noguchi was assigned to work on marketing Toyota in America. He executed his own solutions, which are the topic of this book, in an attempt to grasp the hearts and minds of the American customer.

WHEN IN ROME, DO AS THE ROMANS

Japanese people have maintained a thinking habit of "when you are placed in a township, follow the customs of the township." The opposite can be seen in Western countries as demonstrated by their approach to colonial rule where they erased all of the original culture of their colonies and implanted their own Western culture, which was a part of the thinking habit of Western countries. For example, in Japan, the first cars imported from the United States were all equipped with left steering wheels. This comes as a result of manufacturers' pursuit of economies of scale and ignoring the consumers in the marketplace.

Whenever we move into a new market we find unique rules, regulations, laws, and customs that are inherently local. Toyota always tries to comply with any rules and regulations of its respective markets in order to preserve the local cultures by following their customs while simultaneously creating employment and expanding demand. Take, for example, the American market. Toyota introduced cars that were free from customers' complaints, cars with better fuel mileage, cars with roomier interiors, and customized larger-sized cars for special markets like Texas. However, for Europe, Toyota offered cars with more emphasis on mobility such as driving performance and quick response. For colder places or high-elevation markets, local Toyota dealers and Toyota Engineering (local) worked closely with Toyota in Japan to design and market appropriate cars as needed in their respective markets offering specially designed variations. All these efforts were a part of winning over customer satisfaction. Toyota attempted to satisfy local needs. Instead of using the conventional marketing theory of selling mass-produced and identical cars to global markets, Toyota has innovated marketing by producing and selling cars that satisfy local conditions, fitting what was desired by the local market. This is the primary marketing innovation that Toyota introduced.

As for its view of the future, Akio Toyoda, current president of Toyota, responded to an interview by *Nikkei-Financial Times* by saying, "I know that other big players of the automobile industry are focusing their strategy on eco-cars. Nissan is looking at electric cars. Daimler is focused on fuel cell cars. But at Toyota we invested about $10 billion annually for R&D in wider applications of various eco-cars that will meet the diversified requirements of various regions throughout the world." He is not simply focused on the convenience of a manufacturer, but he is literally focusing on incorporating the thinking habit of when you are placed in a township, follow the customs of the township.

GLOBAL STRATEGY AND ANTITRUST LAWS

In any country that Toyota moves into, it must respect unique rules, laws, and regulations as well as local customs. Toyota must pay special attention to relevant laws. Antitrust laws, in particular, may cause international tensions and violations may result in big losses. In the United States, we know there have been many cases of large penalties, as much as several billion yen or hundreds of millions of U.S. dollars resulting from the strict enforcement of antirust laws. This mistake is referred to as a "mistake of the first kind." It is the result of the non-observance of regulations and it is a malpractice that is considered to not be justifiable.

When General Motors, then the world's biggest car maker, launched a new joint-venture company with Toyota, which is still Japan's biggest joint venture ever, U.S. antitrust laws were strictly adhered to before any approvals were made for fear of any damage to a third party. For instance, at the negotiation table with GM or at the occasion of policy decision discussions among top management officers on both sides, it was mandated to have lawyers present without exception and they were required to submit the minutes of these meetings to Washington. At all executive-level meetings, all meeting procedures were recorded in the minutes with every attendant's signature. The minutes were sent to the top administration and legal affairs officers to check every conversation during the meeting to make sure there was never any violation of antitrust laws. The U.S. government was focused on confirming that any decision made by this GM–Toyota joint venture would not result in disadvantaging other U.S. car business concerns. This was the result of a specific request made by the chairman of Chrysler Motor.

WHILE HOLDING ON TO PATRIOTISM, BECOME A DYED-IN-THE-WOOL CITIZEN OF THE COUNTRY

Both in culture and business, a practice of "when you are placed in a township, follow the customs of the township" requires that your behavior identifies you as a local citizen. This is considered critical when attempting to have your customers become good fans of Toyota. In the heyday of the Japan–U.S. trade disputes, Japanese cars were considered to be responsible for robbing jobs from American workers and Toyota experienced challenges because of these biased views. It was at this point that Toyota felt it had to "become a local citizen to full extent" and author Noguchi jumped whole-heartedly into this challenge.

An episode describing this appears in the book *Mirai-wo-Shinji, Ippozutsu* [Step by Step, with a Belief in the Future] by Shoichiro Toyoda, former chairman of Toyota Motor, and published by the *Nihon Keizai Shimbun Press*. He states,

> Our people from Toyota, Japan intentionally chose new housing in local neighborhoods instead of flocking together and creating our own small Japanese community, because they wished to integrate themselves into their new American community. Fujio Cho, the second president of Toyota Motor Manufacturing built a Karaoke room at his residence and invited his American friends inside and outside of the company in an attempt to foster local friendships. Kentucky is a land of Stephen Collins Foster, the father of American home music and Cho sang "My Old Kentucky Home" in English, joined by his friends. This occurred because Toyota had sent a Karaoke set with *Goheimochi*, a popular local snack from back home to Kan Higashi the then–vice president of NUMMI. All of this was done in an effort to deepen friendships and to increase communication with the local community in a positive way.

OFFERING A NEW DREAM
TO THE CITIZENS OF THE COUNTRY

To gain cultural citizenship you need to offer something to the citizens that they cannot live without. In the case of Toyota, it was to supply them with better cars and improved service. It was not enough to provide the world top-quality cars at affordable prices filled with features, as Toyota did in Japan to the local customers there. Toyota's mission was and still is to offer the best cars along with top-class customer satisfaction. Toyota's marketing strategy aims to satisfy customer expectations, such as zero emission of carbon dioxide, smaller and affordable hybrid vehicles, plug-in hybrid cars, fuel cell vehicles, no traffic accidents by using a electronic assist system, and autonomous driving cars. When we succeed in offering cars without emissions as well as systems to enhance their health as a token of our commitment to the value of every citizen, we will get even closer to being recognized as a member of a local community. These types of strategic initiatives lead to Toyota's strength in "product innovation," thereby bringing out something that the host country had not previously experienced.

CREATING A SPIRIT THAT GIVES BACK TO SOCIETY

Next in importance after getting accepted as a cultural citizen is to strengthen and grow the local market by sharing Toyota's success with them. This is accomplished by expanding employment and by giving back benefits to the local marketplace, like the full use of Toyota's human resources, technologies, and financial strength. It is critical to have mutual benefits for both the local community and Toyota. When you succeed in building win–win relationships, your business will succeed in having long-term survival. This idea is different from the conventional way of marketing and selling cars. Toyota employs this approach for the benefit of every recipient country that it becomes involved in. The American business model, often referred to as the "Vulture Company," which became widespread in Japan during the postbubble economy, has very little chance of sustainability.

MINDFULNESS IN PROCUREMENT

In order to build a mutually beneficial win–win relationship, Toyota adopted a policy of utilizing local resources, such as people and suppliers, and sharing the realization that we are all in the same boat together. Toyota focuses on fair competition and on taking advantage of local content based on the principle of "local produce, local consumption" attempting to enhance and grow local suppliers in both quality and quantity. For instance, Toyota found that typical American parts manufacturers are good at selling their products but rarely get involved in the design stage with a focus on meeting customer requirements. Toyota introduced its concept of "design in" to involve parts suppliers in the design stage. Toyota engineers were called in from Japan to meet with local suppliers who were assembled at a hotel. They initiated the joint development of certain parts in order to enhance the synergy of working together.

The thinking habit of seeking for the unique differences at any given point in time leads to the creation of overwhelming synergistic strength. The first secret ingredient of Toyota's strength is, therefore, its own thinking habit to seek and sustain its uniqueness.

TOYOTA'S GLOBAL MARKETING STRATEGY: SECRET INGREDIENT #1

Principle of Breakthrough Thinking—Assume your problems and opportunity are one of a kind. Do not emulate or copy everything.

Conventional wisdom—Look for successful case examples, find similar business models of the past and copy them. Many businesses are searching for successful case examples. Their thinking habit is to follow a leader from which they can adopt their ideas.

At Toyota—So far in this book, Toyota has established its thinking habit to seek uniqueness, as shown in the following instances:

- It did not copy other leading companies such as Ford and GM. "Just-in-time" is a Toyota original.

- Adapt to the local environment of a subject country and use that to identify who, where, and when to identify and apply effective solutions.
- "Do as the Romans do" for everything related to culture and society.

Question for Reflection

We see two approaches to marketing strategy in the automobile industry: the first is focused on overall cost reduction by assembling universally identical designs, and the second one is focused on the pursuit of local market–oriented cars. Discuss the most appropriate marketing strategy. Why is it appropriate?

3

Secret Ingredient #2: Just-in-Time Information Collection—The Purposeful Information Principle

THE NEGATIVE EFFECT OF THE INTERNET

The Internet is changing our world with ever-increasing volumes of information and data shared through the Web. Both e-commerce and search capabilities enable us to get what we need when we need it. However, not everything about the Web is positive. Sometimes we have to wonder if our world is really stepping forward. Instead we cannot help but say that we are stepping backward in some areas, such as in the problem of privacy leakage, rampant virus infections, cyberattacks, paralysis by network failures, growing net crimes, anticipated hacking, and technology homicide.

The worst effect of the Internet is that we are faced with the growing danger of information confusion. We have stopping thinking while at the same time we are drowning in a flood of data and information. The authors experienced this behavior while lecturing at their respective universities. For example, when assigning students to perform research on what today's women in their 40s like most, the students immediately access their laptops to start searching and finding articles that they can copy and paste into their reports. The authors call this kind of research "copy-and-paste reporting." As the student's ability to search, copy, and paste has been improved, they seldom employ their own brain to think, wonder, and create on their own. None of the students would go out to ask women in their 40s what they like. They blindly believe whatever is posted on the Internet. Astonishingly, 90% of the current generation of students have been trained to cut out someone else's sentences without the original author's consent when they are submitting their reports, with very little of their own creative thinking. When students submit their reports, this book's authors often find almost identical contents in multiple students' work. They all copied from the same place. Even when creating their graduation theses, the same phenomenon occurs. Even though the students are instructed to "go out into the field and gather live information," more students take the easy way out and extract other researchers' findings from the Web, cut and paste it, and use it to complete their own work. A professor's efforts in reviewing graduation thesis work have become a struggle with "net-dependent plagiarism" as well as the "copy-and-paste thesis." This occurs in both Japan and the United States. Both find that most theses are "pasted plagiarism," even at the college and university levels. Those individuals who have become accustomed to using the Internet's virtual world have not realized that they are in danger of suffering from a sickness of emulating only the appearance of creativity while ignoring the process of creative thinking. This thinking habit destroys the essential meaning of creativity.

THE EXPANDING VIRTUAL WORLD

The lack of creative thinking has not only affected students. For example, consider the case of the medical doctor. Traditionally, doctors saw the human body of a patient holistically using such common practices as checking facial color and the throat, pressing one's belly, hearing the heart beat using a stethoscope, and so on. But today's doctors look first at the data found on computers rather than their patients. An increasing number of medical service cases are dependent on the partial data of a patient's health, instead of using a holistic view, in making their judgments about treatment. It is often said that the growing number of errors in prescribing medication and treatment are attributed to this data-centered approach of medical service, which is solely based on virtual data.

Another example can be found in our government agencies. We find a similar tendency there as well. For example, look at organizations in charge of international assistance. Just 30 years ago, officials used to work one-on-one with their counterparts in recipient countries. However, as their budgets decreased and their scope of work increased, those same officials moved away from the frontline and instead they resorted to searching through the data output from their computers. Recently this has caused a lot of regret from the staffers of these organizations. The data approach has caused disastrous scenes in Africa when the staffers' only experience is virtual. They see their funds have often been appropriated and misused. They often complain that they need to be at the scene in order to creatively find appropriate solutions. They want to think creatively at the scene of the crisis in order to find the best solutions and to support the people in these developing countries. This cannot be accomplished by only staring at data.

Needless to say, the same thing occurs in corporations. Their office floors are filled with individuals fighting through computer data from numerous virtual sources. Consequently, since all companies use the same data, most companies create identical corporate strategies. For example, when achievement-based pay systems are in fashion, they all snatch them up. More companies are forecasting their futures using lagging indicators as an extension of their past based on the same virtual data. They set their goals by using data to break down their future vision and use that to define future results. They run their operations and their entire business without knowing what is really happening on the frontlines of their business.

The ongoing Internet revolution will lead to making data and information more virtual. Increased "virtualization" makes it harder for us to identify the essence of everything we do, resulting in a decrease in the possibility of achieving unique solutions. We need to realize that this is a trap that we are all falling into. We need to consider why Toyota's thinking habit emphasizes the gemba ("go and observe"), which stresses "going to the real place." Why do they consider this as more and more critical?

RUNNING IN FUTILITY: GEMBA-ISM

The language of *gemba-shugi*, also known as "go and observe" or "hands-on policy," is being applied in various ways in numerous industries. Unfortunately, this concept is misunderstood and largely misused. The following story is typical of the widespread misuse.

The president of an unnamed company who was an advocate of the hands-on approach decided to travel to all his factory locations throughout the country in order to personally guide their operations. Plant managers, hearing about this new policy, considered this to be a big event and directed their organizations to make elaborate preparations to welcome the president. They did a thorough cleaning, tidying and removing of unnecessary items. They arranged everything, even to the extreme of having mock visits in preparation for the real event. Even the plant operators were instructed to practice welcoming the boss in advance so that the visit would come off flawlessly. Then the plant managers waited for the big boss's visit.

The day of the visit arrived. The president, after his tour and mentorship, was impressed. He announced "job well done," and went home but without looking below the surface at the real operational performance of the factory. He enjoyed his trip including the customary night's stay at the favorite restaurant-hotel of the plant manager, paid for by the company. The hotel offered its best in hospitality to the boss's party, as the company was its best customer.

How do you feel about this story? If you were there, what would you do? This president looked at a staged and showcased factory in a fake virtual world rather than seeing it as it really operates. The president's attempt to focus on the principle of being hands-on turned out to be mirage. As demonstrated by the plant manager in this story, the recipient side tries its best to glorify the true shape of the operation. This results in erroneous evaluations made by top management.

It would be more appropriate to visit one of your plants without any forewarning or announcement to see the production lines in action and to talk with the frontline associates. Do this without any preparation. Stay at a hotel that does not have a connection with the company. It is essential to get a clear understanding of the hearts and minds of all your stakeholders and consumers.

One hit television series in Japan was a drama called *Abarenbo Shogun*, a story about the eighth Shogun during the Tokugawa years named Yoshimune Tokugawa. This supreme ruler of the nation disguised himself as a rank-and-file samurai, Shinnosuke Tokuda, and wandered around the town of Edo (currently Tokyo) to judge whether his government policies were effective. He looked for the effects of policies on the day-to-day affairs of the people. He also looked for signs of conspiracy. Does this sound familiar to what we have already been talking about? It is! Toyota's hands-on policy was inherited from the thinking habits of the Tokugawa years.

In Toyota, there is a famous story about its hands-on policy called "Ohno's Circle." This is the hands-on policy that Taiichi Ohno implemented in the factory. He instructed his subordinates that if the line stopped, then they needed to go to the actual spot of the failure, draw a 1 meter circle, and stand there until the group finds the true cause of the failure by asking "Why? Why? Why? Why? Why? And so on." This is Toyota's hands-on policy.

TOYOTA'S HEADQUARTERS ARE IN THE GEMBA (ON THE FACTORY FLOOR)

Watching the television series mentioned in the previous section reminds us of the important fact that Toyota's main office lies in a small city of Toyota itself. This emphasizes Toyota's thinking habit and makes it meaningful. Common sense would dictate that you anticipate that a large enterprise like Toyota Motor Company would have its main offices in Tokyo. Many corporations moved their head offices to Tokyo in compliance with this generally accepted approach. However, Toyota, breaking from the norm, still keeps its head office in Toyota City, rejecting what others would consider to be common sense. Toyota was once described as maintaining its own version of the Monroe Doctrine. It is often poked fun at by its critics as being its own "country kingdom."

However, considering how Toyota is applying its hands-on policy, we must conclude that its head office, where decisions are made, needs to be at the location of its operations. Top managers of manufacturing enterprises should do their thinking where production occurs. That way their thinking becomes hands-on since they would be present at the location of the action. In following the hands-on philosophy, the head office of Toyota Motors must be located in Toyota City, not Tokyo. To them it is nonsense that so many enterprise heads are located in Tokyo. From the viewpoint of the thinking habits built around the hands-on principle, matters relevant to the government should be decided in Tokyo, whereas operational functions, like global marketing, should be headquartered near a major international airport. That would be the natural hands-on conclusion. Currently, Toyota Motor has its hub of all global business strategy located close to the Nagoya Station, just 35 minutes away from the Chubu International Airport.

Toyota does not emulate other players but has adopted its own strategy to gather relevant data and information at the place closest to the place of operations, in compliance with its objectives. Those critics who insist that Toyota should move its head office to Tokyo and who criticize it as creating its own Toyota Monroe Doctrine are simply too near-sighted and do not see the big picture. Taking the perspective of the thinking habits, we can see an entirely different point of view.

THE GENCHI/GEMBUTSU/GEMBA-ISM PRINCIPLE

Taiichi Ohno (1912–1990) roughly challenged the Toyota employees over and over again with the same declarations:

> "Make solutions at the real place, the place where the work is happening. See the actual activity. Only then can you identify the essence of its operation."
>
> "Don't look at the appearance but see the essence hidden inside the activity."
>
> "Don't see with your eyes but with your mind."
>
> "Why, why, why, why, why? Repeat the question over and over in order to identify the fundamental cause. Only then can you identify the root cause and find a solution."

He used these statements to emphasize that the most practical information about any activity is only found by going to the actual location of the activity. We need to go to the "real place" in order to find the real object of the real situations. Compare his thinking habits with the previously discussed copy–paste reporting thinking habits focused on virtual information, as we previously compared them to the university students. It is quite illuminating to understand that Toyota's thinking habits represented by Ohno emphasize that we should think through the process in order to reach the "essence" of the process and to identify "fundamentally unique" solutions.

We need to stress the perspective that in Toyota's thinking habits, data and information should be gathered to achieve wisdom about the actual activity that is occurring (the real thing at the real place). It is hoped that the reader finds that what Toyota says of *gemba*, *gembutsu*, and *genjitsu* (go to the real place, see the real thing, and identify the real facts) calls for in-depth thinking as a part of its thinking habit.

The following episode is from the late Soichiro Honda (1906–1991), the founder of Honda Motor, not Toyota. He highlighted several points about the potential danger of obsessive data or information collection as follows:

1. Danger of being incorrectly swayed by data. Data (information) is just a means for giving direction. It is not the solution.
2. Danger of mixing necessary and unnecessary data (information).
3. Danger of overlooking the same-result-causing data (information) missing the fact that they have different causes.
4. Danger of self-believing that you identified something and accomplished something by compiling a document. The document is not the objective. Be careful that you don't think you have accomplished anything by creating a document or by simply collecting data (information).

Soichiro Honda's point about "data and information as being just a means to an end" is very important. Data and information represent the objective. They are just inputs toward a solution. Traditional conventional thinking suggests that a job starts with data and information collection. This is incorrect. We should not start with the means to the end. Rather, we should start by looking at the essence or the true objective of our effort. Toyota's thinking habits call for visiting the actual location of the item being studied. We need to see the actual thing. We need to use our mind and think through what is actually occurring, instead of starting with data and information collection. Under conventional thinking we would start thinking only after getting the information or data. However, when you properly start thinking from the essence or objective, you start thinking without information.

In medicine we now see that doctors make their diagnosis using the data output of computers or the medical equipment. But the human body is very complex, which makes it difficult to identify the real cause of any problems without looking at the big picture. Accordingly, it is more critical now than ever to obtain new thinking habits when doing a diagnosis. The entangled human organs and their functions comprise a larger integrated system that cannot be observed by simply looking at the data and the resulting information.

In traditional conventional thinking, we confuse the making of a document, thinking that this is the creation of a solution. Problem solution or idea creation requires that we achieve an objective, which is not the compilation of a document. Such jobs as documentation or the pinpointing of a problem have nothing to do with the essence of what we are working on. Toyota's thinking habits focus on genchi-gembutu-gemba as its core and is necessary in order to create solutions.

The authors do not deny the existence and value of virtual realms, including the Internet. Rather, we recognize the dangers in the overabundance of data and information resulting in confusion and making it harder to identify the essence and roots of a situation. Defining a problem or creating new ideas by putting them into digital form biases the perspective of the analyst and distorts the vision of the essence of a situation. Toyota's thinking habits are becoming more important with its focus on observance: going to the real place, seeing the real thing, and identifying the real facts.

The authors would like to quote the words of Kiichiro Toyoda, father of Shoichiro, from his book *Believe in the Future, Step by Step*. His father told him to "wash your hands three times a day," implying that the full-fledge engineer's hands ought to be dirty from such things as oil or metal chips. They need to be involved in the process and have hands-on experience. Toyota emphasizes a thinking of "genchi-gembutsu" before judging anything. We cannot judge until we have seen the situation with our own eyes. The idea comes from Kiichiro's statement to place "priority on 'real place.'" These words of Kiichiro represent the starting point of Toyota's thinking, focused on the real place.

IMAGINATION IS GREATER THAN KNOWLEDGE AND INFORMATION

With the ongoing Internet revolution, the saying "Information and knowledge means strength" is becoming increasingly true. Many people are finding it challenging to identify more information. The authors do not deny this trend. However, we want the reader to know that there is an alternative viewpoint. For example, Albert Einstein, the creator of the theory of relativity, said, "The power to image is more important than knowledge (information)." What he meant by this is that we should "imagine a perfect state before collecting information." This is often referred to as "Einstein's search for a sweetheart." He did not discover this new theory of relativity by using conventional methods of information collection and analysis. This new theory did not follow a conventional theoretical model for idea creation. No one denies the power of information and knowledge.

However, merely having information or knowledge does not mean power. Information, data, and knowledge as well as know-how of the past and present can be used to exert power only when you know how to use them. The power that we are referring to is the ability to appropriately and meaningfully use your knowledge and information. Henry Ford said, "What you are considering becomes feasible as you can imagine an ideal state in an explicit manner." He called for the ability to creatively imagine ideas and solutions before executing. He drove toward achieving results by exploiting knowledge and information. However, we are witnessing that more people are simply responding to biased information just like those copy-and-paste papers created by students who pay little attention to the real place where the information comes from. That is why we feel that the capacity for imagination is rapidly decreasing.

Looking at Toyota's thinking habits, especially its hands-on principle, we can understand that this hands-on principle is empowering Toyota. Taiichi Ohno instructed, "Go to the real place before collecting information. Then repeat asking the question 'why' five times seeking the root cause." Seeking and observing real activities allows us to see possibilities that are not easily visible (seeing in the mind). It allows us to see causes in processes and help them become visible. This mechanism empowers the capacity of imagination for Toyota employees and it also strengthens the thinking habit, allowing individuals to become creative thinkers. One more Henry Ford quote is, "Move forward and move on, even if you are not aware of all the facts. In the process of moving forward and taking action, the facts become comprehensible." That is exactly the same as the thinking habit of Taiichi Ohno, who said, "Go to the actual scene. Then, while asking 'why,' 'why,' and 'why' you will see the facts and the true causes."

Kiichiro Toyoda never forgot to pursue his "sweetheart," which was the production of passenger cars using Japanese indigenous technologies. Right after the end of WWII, leaving operations of the Toyota factories to Eiji Toyoda, Kiichiro stayed in Tokyo to observe the occupation forces in Japan and to assist the Japanese government in creating the country's future. Kiichiro, therefore, executed his version of data and information collection at the appropriate time, only collecting the necessary data in just the required amount.

This book refers to Kiichiro's way of information collection by the unique name of "just-in-time information collection." This thinking habit, thinking in terms of a just-in-time approach, has been inherited in a nonstop and continuous way from the days of the Tokugawa feuds to today's Toyota.

APPLYING GEMBA-ISM WHEN PIONEERING A NEW MARKET

The Toyota approach to emphasize the three-gen principle (genchi-gembutsu-gemba) was first rooted in production, but later it was boldly applied to Toyota's global marketing approach. Initially, Toyota observed the principle of appropriate information collection where it started by creating an objective marketing strategy. Then it determined what information should be gathered. That was followed by stepping into "the real place, dealing with the actual thing, and identify the difference between the essence and the real thing." Following the philosophy of "using your feet to walk through a market," Toyota tried to identify the needs of subject countries from the viewpoint of the local citizens by looking at business customs, identifying individual preferences, and considering human sensitivities in order to identify the types of vehicles that would be welcomed and which would satisfy local customers. For instance, in Southern California and Nice, France, where marine sports are popular, they workers experienced that lifestyle. They tried to get along with the local people and learn first-hand what was desired. This information was sent to the Toyota Design Lab so that the findings could be used to develop their favorite cars. This type of data, gained by "using your feet to walk through a market" was the foundation for the Toyota methodology. Toyota backed this with statistics, buyer surveys, and customer feedback to create the finalized version of its marketing strategy for the appropriate car model and then put it into practice. Thus, Toyota's global marketing strategy was prepared using a combination of market information and statistics.

Shozo Hibino, one of the authors of this book, had a similar experience not specifically related with Toyota. He had worked as a consultant for Samsung of South Korea and had offered his guidance to a then-fledgling Korean business helping it adopt a unique marketing strategy. It was based on a similar local market–oriented approach in which Samsung employees were sent on location to the relevant countries. There they experienced local living conditions and came up with the most suitable understanding for the local cultures. Samsung immediately put these learnings into practice. Since then, the company has been successful in exploring markets all over the world.

WHAT CREATES A SHEEP-LIKE PHENOMENON?

Today, both improved transportation, the Internet, and data collection technologies have resulted in the higher mobility of everything including materials, money, information, and people. These changes have occurred around the globe. Our world of the twenty-first century is experiencing an unprecedented phenomenon. An advanced Internet means a greater influence in areas beyond the economy, such as influencing people's minds, including their deep psyche. We are seeing cases where people are moving in a uniform direction at a global level. Hibino named this the "sheep phenomenon." At a sheep ranch, the barking dogs move sheep uniformly in a similar direction and the sheep move without thinking (Figure 3.1).

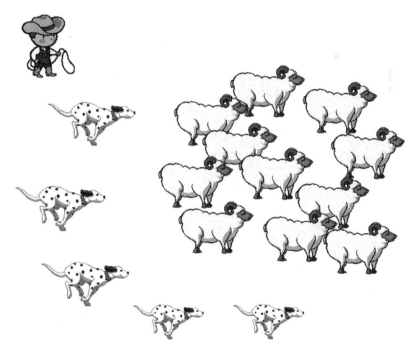

FIGURE 3.1
Herding sheep.

Sometimes they end up rushing only to fall off a cliff. It is not exaggerated for us to label our twenty-first century as an age where we are producing reactive people who just respond to the "barking dogs" of information without stopping to think for themselves.

This sheep phenomenon can be applied to the global marketing efforts in most companies. For instance, Americans use the "joint survey" where they apply the same methodology to every company every year as they compare and gauge the degree of customer satisfaction. J.D. Power, for example, contacts new car buyers after 6 months by telephone to identify their level of customer satisfaction. The car consultancy can then compare each car brand to identify the best performer in terms of customer satisfaction. They use this data to improve their strategy for car assemblers following the principle of real places, real cars, and real customers. *Consumer Reports* buys brand new cars from each automobile maker and evaluates and publishes its data on lifetime service performance annually based on their actual mileage and maintenance cost. When participating in these surveys and considering who achieves the number one position in customer satisfaction, brand image is significantly improved. Toyota cars have achieved the highest levels of customer satisfaction in all of these surveys.

In a nutshell, it is Toyota's secret ingredient #2, which focuses on not seeking solutions after only collecting and analyzing huge amounts of data and information, but to first focus on the Toyota thinking habit of just-in-time information collection where we only collect the essential and necessary information in only the required volume in order to formulate the most appropriate business strategy. This is all based on the genchi-gembutsu-gemba principle of going to the real place, dealing with the actual thing, and identifying the essence from the real thing.

TOYOTA'S GLOBAL MARKETING STRATEGY: SECRET INGREDIENT #2

A principle of Breakthrough Thinking—When working toward a solution, collect the minimum amount of data. Only collect data that is relevant toward the objective. Data collection should only generate relevant and timely information that is specific to the issue at hand.

To apply Toyota's thinking habit, this principle can be referred to as "just-in-time information collection."

Conventional wisdom—In order to precisely identify a problem, it is necessary to gather as much information as possible related to the problem. This results in an obsession to collect any and all data with a special focus on how or what the competition is doing.

At Toyota—Toyota recommends that the use of data collection and information collection should be limited to what is necessary in shaping a better solution. This should occur at the location of the desired outcome. Rather than collecting and analyzing vast amounts of data used to identify a problem, it suggests that we "go and observe" what is happening at the location of the issue being analyzed. Toyota emphasizes "visualized" information collection "on location" of the actual object being analyzed in various ways, both by individuals and by groups.

Question for Reflection

In today's world, which is flooded with information, we are challenged to create a new strategic marketing plan. Describe how you would gather and analyze information in the creation of this plan.

4

Secret Ingredient #3: A Professional Systems Architecture—The Systems Principle

THE SECRET OF THE TOKUGAWA THINKING HABITS

The Tokugawa shogunate turned out to be an exceptional form of government in that it kept Japanese society peaceful and stable for over 265 years. Rulers of most other countries of the world failed to sustain their government structure following conquest. The linchpins of this long-lasting administration can be found in Tokugawa's own thinking habits and how they were applied in the creation of "systems." The thinking habits of the early Tokugawa shoguns Ieyasu and Iemitsu Tokugawa, who directly inherited their thinking habits from the original Mikawa warriors, was quite astonishing.

There were many leaders before those two outstanding shoguns who had ruled the country by force. However, after winning a civil war, the founding fathers of the Tokugawa first used their wisdom and then focused on systems in order to rule the entire country. For example, this can be seen in the system of Sankin Kotai (alternating attendance at the capital), which worked effectively to contain any attempt to revolt. The shogunate demanded every provincial lord to pay a state visit to Edo (current Tokyo). This requirement resulted in these lords alternatively living in Edo and in their home country every other year, while their wives and children were ordered to permanently stay in Edo. This process started when Ieyasu Tokugawa was in power, and the third generation of Ieyasu Tokugawa finished using this system and kept it in place until the late nineteenth century.

Additional benefits of this system are numerous, ranging from minimizing the opportunities for revolts by effectively taking the lords' families as hostage, to the economic significance of loading potential revolutionary lords with expenses and thereby financially reducing their power. The system also promoted the creation of townships along the trail road, supporting foot traffic. This was still a time when people used to walk whenever they journeyed. This helped to establish the Tokugawa thinking habits into a nationwide system. These original thinking habits from a tiny Mikawa community were also adapted into Toyota, and the company is cited for its genius at creating systems. The prime example of successful systems is demonstrated in the Toyota Production System (TPS), where parts flow smoothly and are transferred between processes using kanbans.

A "BUILDING STRUCTURES" GENIUS SUPPORTS TOYOTA'S ARCHITECTURE

The founders of the Tokugawa methodology worked hard to create a system using their creative wisdom, and these systems supported the subsequent rulings by the Tokugawa shogunate. The Sankin Kotai was just one such system. In order to prevent invasion by other countries, Tokugawa decided to close off Japan except for a small section in Nagasaki. This section was used to collect information from the Western nations. This system of isolation still monitored the outside world, while at the same time keeping Japan safe from invasion and allowing internal prosperity to grow during those years.

Toyota shares similar thinking habits. Let us take a look at the system that is today called the Toyota Production System (TPS) and which is supporting Toyota. This system is based on a concept of "going to the preceding process workstation and receiving parts in exchange for an empty kanban." Building on this basic system concept, Toyota conceived various additional systems. For example, the andon system, where operators stop the line and turn on a light whenever a defect is detected, and the leveling system, which creates a congestion-free flow of production. These systems are used by all employees, empowering them in their job functions. Toyota has proven its ability to make systems. Sharing this thinking habit with others caused many people who were connected with Toyota to dedicate themselves to creating additional appropriate systems in numerous areas throughout the company's operations.

THE WISDOM OF USING BUILDING STRUCTURES IN THE ALLIED FORCES OF TOKUGAWA AND NOBUNAGA

Nobunaga Oda, another big name during the civil war years, was not connected with the Mikawa clans since he originated from the region of Owari. However, he was good at creating systems. His goal was the conquest of Japan. He looked to the future and used his ingenuity to win major battles. Ieyasu Tokugawa, who joined together with Nobunaga Oda in order to survive the turbulent years, is believed to share Nobunaga's thinking habits. When considering the alliance between Nobunaga Oda and Ieyasu Tokugawa we are reminded of the one between GM and Toyota. After the first oil crisis in the 1970s and the subsequent price hike of fuel, Toyota looked toward future growth, while GM focused on its position as the biggest car manufacturer in the world. Although Toyota looked smaller than GM in the 1980s, Toyota maintained its focus on competition and collaboration when working with the American giant. The on-again, off-again relationship between the two reminds us of the thinking habits of Ieyasu Tokugawa and how their previous small feud resulted in an alliance.

One example of Nobunaga Oda's beliefs can be found in "always being ahead of the time." This was incorporated in his use of firearms. Musket rifles were introduced to Japan in 1543 by Portuguese seamen who drifted onto Tanegashima Island. Two original rifles were copied by a local sword blacksmith and his new rifles were called Tanegashima rifles. They became the Japanese modern firearms. This new weapon was easily diffused all over Japan. By 1555, 12 years after the arrival of the original Portuguese guns, Shingen Takeda used 300 Tanegashima-model guns at the battle of the Asahiyama castle in Shinano country.

Fighting battles using guns triggered a significant innovation in how to fight more effectively. Up to then, fighting a battle meant one-on-one fighting between warriors who initiated the fight. They started by first introducing themselves. For example, they would say, "I am the distinguished fighter Uzaemon of the Mikawa country." The new technique of using guns to do battle occurred at the battle of Nagashino between the coalition forces of the Oda and Tokugawa troops against Takeda's cavalry, which had a reputation for being the strongest. The Oda–Tokugawa forces won the battle, previously considered to be unwinnable for them, by using conventional wisdom and traditional methods. They successfully took advantage of the new guns by creating a system focused on optimizing the use of the guns in their unique geography. When the Takeda cavalry were slow to attack the castle of Nagashino, the Oda–Tokugawa coalition forces built a makeshift fort in the Shidaragahama pass, a narrow pass that was used to lure the Takeda horse soldiers. While waiting for the incoming army, the defenders developed a new way to fire their guns, referred to as "three-stage firing." Rifle troops were divided into three groups and synchronized so that the 3000 Tanegashima guns could be fired cyclically and in turn.

Using this three-stage shooting technique, the second squad would prepare themselves by lighting their guns while the first squad was firing. The third squad would be loading their guns during this time. Repeating this, they could pour bullets "without delay" at the incoming horse soldiers of the Takeda army and deprive them of their mobility. The three-stage firing technique is equivalent to today's machine gun rapid-fire shooting. The "curtain of fire" approach used by machine guns against an approaching enemy in order to annihilate them was created by the Oda–Tokugawa coalition forces. In the end, the battle was an overwhelming victory for the creative soldiers. Using the previous traditional mode of doing battle where a warrior would first identify himself by saying, "I am the renowned warrior of …" was focused on the capability and performance of the individual, whereas three-stage firing did not depend on the performance of an outstanding warrior. It focused on the continuous barrage of bullets as being the key to annihilating the opponent. This was a significant innovation in battle strategies.

An important note that we need to pay attention to in this battle is that the thinking habits of the warriors looked for innovative strategies that would allow them to beat a superior force. They organized systems like forcing the enemy to travel through narrow passageways and the curtain of fire generated by having three teams of shooters to outmaneuver the enemy. Their systems focused on generating a winning strategy that would compensate for their short handedness. This strategy turned out to be more strategically powerful than just the individual use of guns.

In Toyota, we often find groups or teams of people who very naturally work and study together to solve problems, as shown in the use of the practice of *jishu ken* (voluntary study teams). Toyota has inherited the thinking habits of "strategic systems building" from the old Mikawa warriors who demonstrated greater strength by creating an integrated system strategy. The strength of Toyota comes from its use of thinking habits focused on building integrated systems.

THE SECRET OF JUST-IN-TIME

The story of how the strongest Takeda horse soldiers were able to be defeated by a group of backcountry militants from Mikawa can be applied to Toyota who also defeated the strongest players of automobile industry, specifically General Motors (GM) and Ford. This book emphasizes this unique approach focused on "strong bypassing power" (the ability to leapfrog ahead) as a key thinking habit.

When Kiichiro Toyoda started producing automobiles in the 1930s, Americans' productivity levels were extremely high, over nine times that of Japan. It was easy to conclude that Japan's chances of creating their own automotive industry were poor indeed. Additionally, Kiichiro was stuck in the "nothing-nothing syndrome," as reviewed in Chapter 1, and under this condition it would have been impossible to grow his fledging car assembly shop into a world-class competitor. However, Kiichiro inherited the thinking habits of the Mikawa people and boldly faced this challenge. He recognized the need to create a unique Japanese approach (his own system) with higher productivity and lower cost in order to compete with the advanced Western automobile competitors. This becomes a key message that cannot be overlooked. An ordinary thinking approach would suggest that Toyota would say, "We should copy the Ford way of doing things since this American company is performing superior to us." But Kiichiro did not follow this ordinary, traditional way of thinking.

The Ford Motor Company, the front-runner in those days, believed that the best approach for production was to use a system of mass production. This system produced more cars by using an assembly-line approach with conveyer belts. This caused Ford to keep a large volume of inventory, which was stored in large warehouses at each process location. Kiichiro Toyoda, however, was not satisfied with this approach. He searched for ideas that would allow him to compete with the advanced Western car manufacturers. His search resulted in a new systems approach that was the complete opposite of his competitors. He advocated an approach focused on producing what was needed, when it was needed, and in the quantity it was needed. This new system received the name "just-in-time." His son, Shoichiro, wrote in his book *Step by Step; Believing in the Future* that his father had cautioned, "Those individuals who progressed because of their own hard work possessed within themselves the power for progress. But those individuals who search for knowledge the easy way, by simply looking for and copying other people's work lack the power and vigor to stand out as progressive thinkers." The authors of this book hope that its readers pay attention to Kiichiro's thinking habits that value "trying even when you think something is impossible" and "face the challenge and compete with your predecessors and your competition, not by imitating them, but by searching for and finding new systems approaches. Think through the essence of what you are trying to accomplish and leapfrog ahead. Don't imitate and hope imitation will allow you to bypass them. That's not good enough."

At the groundbreaking ceremony of the original Koromo Plant in 1935, the words "just-in-time" were used for the first time publically by Kiichiro. He wrote and distributed a new manual spreading the thinking habits of just-in-time across the entire plant.

In that original manual, Kiichiro wrote, "Study and find what our customers want to see reflected in our products," as part of his description about just-in-time. He introduced these new thinking habits hoping to identify the true and latent customer needs and to incorporate these needs into the Toyota production system while continuously looking for opportunities for improving the production with what we now call a "customer satisfaction campaign." Rather than taking the viewpoint of the producer, and instead taking the viewpoint of the user of the automobiles, these thinking habits were applied by the following generations at Toyota.

Americans and the Japanese are different in culture and in the way they use cars. Russia and South Africa differ in weather and climate. What customers consider desirable, lucrative, and attractive in each location is different as well. Toyota cars are now being offered in more models and styles in order to accommodate these varying customer needs and preferences throughout the world.

Kiichiro also wrote, "Search for opportunities to improve products by taking a close look at the production system in addition to focusing on improving the product itself." In the early days, major companies would use preshipment inspections to catch defects. However, Kiichiro stressed, "It is wasteful to discard defective parts after spending a lot of time and effort producing them." His thinking habits evolved into the famous practice of "in-line quality inspections." The origin of Toyota's system to "apply inspection activities at each production step and to stop the production line whenever a defect is detected" came out from the thinking habits of Kiichiro. At this point there was no equivalent thinking habit within Toyota to suggest that quality should be built into the process. For example, when process inspections took place at major parts suppliers within the United States in preparation for NUMMI (New United Motor Manufacturing Inc.), a joint venture between Toyota and GM, in the 1980s, Toyota discovered that most of those suppliers, especially manufacturers of glass, paid little attention to defects during the process. Rejection occurred at the point of final inspection of the vehicle. In the case of large exterior plastic parts, the management and inspection of exterior components were poor allowing, for example, scratches on completed products.

Toyota's thinking habits that quality should be built into the process went far astride of the thinking habits of its current competitors. When tracing the reason for a quality problem, Toyota identifies various failure considerations. Not only can the failures be caused by immature designs or poor production engineering but also other considerations attributable to consumers like improper usage and supplier problems like poor materials. Merely implementing final inspection cannot guarantee the identification of the real cause of a failure. Readers of this book should be familiar with the famous approach by Taiichi Ohno, who advocated repeating asking the question "Why?" five times. This technique is also based on the thinking habits of Kiichiro. The improper Western focus on "management by results" that focuses on the merit system disregards the importance of "management built into the process."

Kiichiro thought that the making of products to satisfy customers requires a systemic approach of doing work that will cover the entire processes, ranging from identifying customers' needs to also include engineering development, design, production, inspection, logistics, services, and maintenance. He also believed the goal of customer satisfaction could not be obtained unless they could improve all processes in a continuous manner. This thinking habit has become the foundation of the current Toyota technique referred to as "Kaizen" (every time improvement, everywhere improvement, every one improvement; continuous improvement).

SYSTEMS STRUCTURE AND SYSTEMS

Both Tokugawa and Toyota could have led the world by their innovative and unique designs of systems. Toyota distinguishes between the creation of the systems structure and the system. The dictionary would give you a definition of a "system" as a structured mechanism or effort. Breakthrough Thinking, however, specifies that "everything is a system." Toyota defines systems structure as part of a system. We need to discuss how Toyota differentiates these concepts.

"Systems structure" is an "architecture or an effort," and it is focused on the intention of people involved in the system. It would be easier to comprehend this as a creative "structure" built on wisdom, insight, and understanding. For instance, let us consider the example of a system structure as the integration of tools like kanban, which Ohno created. This tool facilitates the larger system of just-in-time since it manages inventory and attempts to drive it down to near-zero levels. The kanban system structure represents the creative wisdom of the Toyota team and facilitates the intended results. Therefore, systems structures utilize mechanisms that are engines or tools that drive larger systems. A system without an embedded systems structure cannot function. Embedded system structure mechanisms trigger and start a systems engine and afterward the system automatically moves forward. By repeatedly saying "Reduce inventory!" we cannot achieve a reduction of inventory stock. But once we have embedded a systems structure mechanism focused on reducing the number of monthly kanbans, the engine is started and the entire inventory level of our process reduces automatically without saying anything. Then, a small systems structure mechanism can be used to activate a system that in the end generates the desired results. Toyota's thinking habits constantly focus on maintaining its extraordinary passion of embedding systems structure mechanisms.

Another example of a systems structure trigger mechanism is called the "5S" campaign. It refers to a systems structure mechanism that uses five practices all starting with the letter *S* in the original Japanese: *seiri, seiton, seiso, seiketsu,* and *shitsuke* (the English version of 5S is sort, set in order, shine, standardize, sustain). Practicing all these S words can make your workshop cleaner and more organized, but at the same time it also makes you able to identify wastes that would not normally be visible, like unnecessary inventory. In creating system structure mechanisms, the last *S*, shitsuke, becomes critical. Rather than the usual definition of this word as being to "sustain," Toyota uses the word in reference to "make it a habit." Shitsuke for Toyota is not simply knowledge, but it is the making of a habit. Employees should become so accustomed to any action or activity that they do it without thinking. To make your system workable, you need to embed this habit-forming process. This differs from a system. It is a transformation of the culture, which is the system that we are ultimately after. And shitsuke is the systems structure mechanism or tool that is the trigger for cultural shift. One of the strengths of Toyota is that they incorporate a culture of habits as well as the practice of creating system structure mechanisms as one of their thinking habits.

THE MEANING OF TOYOTA'S KAIZEN SYSTEM

One more concept that we need to look at and which is heavily used by Toyota is its concept of "continuous (perpetual) improvement" and "constant innovation." The concept of systems was a Western idea that the East did not have. Eastern philosophy, without the concept of systems, was focused on being holistic, interlocking or interconnected, and purpose oriented or purpose driven. Western systems theory clarified those ancient oriental thoughts. Put in this context, Toyota inherited the oriental philosophy of the Mikawa people as one of its thinking habits. It was exposed to this thinking practice in order to see everything in a holistic and interlocking way.

Western systems philosophy came to Toyota in 1963 when it learned the concepts of Work Design, which was also incorporated into Breakthrough Thinking. In those early days Toyota was still in the process of creating its Toyota Production System (TPS). The systems principle played a significant role in the formulation of TPS as testified in a book by a Toyota executive in those days titled *Toyota's Systematic Improvement*.

A system can be defined as "an interconnected whole which accomplishes a purpose." Initially it requires a purpose (goal, aim, or function). This involves defining the existential value of the system. When its value disappears, the need for the relevant system will also disappear. When Toyota loses its existential value, Toyota will cease its corporate activity. In a system, every element moves forward in conjunction with one another. Elements cannot exist alone as a system. When one element changes, its interaction with other elements forces them to also change. This leads to Toyota's Kaizen system. Toyota's thinking habits are not aimed at simple improvements. A modification of one point affects other parts or other working stations, which then requires them to have their own Kaizen. Kaizen changes work like a domino effect, triggering "waves of Kaizen" and ever-increasing waves of Kaizen that eventually engulf the entire company. In Toyota, once Kaizen begins, it becomes "Kaizen-aholic," where everyone seems to get triggered and become involved. Kaizen creates a system of interacting changes that acquire Toyota's thinking habits for larger impact and results with an organization-wide effect. This is referred to as "systems Kaizen" and it explains why Kaizen campaigns at companies influenced by conventional reductionist thinking easily become stagnated as they encounter vertically divided organizations.

TOYOTA EMPHASIS ON CONNECTIONS/LINKS

A critical point in a system is its interconnectedness. Just like with dominos where one effects the other, and as seen in system Kaizen, we stress that all subsystems are connected, linked, or inseparable. Toyota's thinking habits have adopted this perspective. America's Ford production system divides all jobs into distinct functions and then dissects them out. Then it attempts to connect them all mechanically using assembly lines and conveyer belts. In the Ford system, there is very little connectivity between the working employees. Their jobs are executed without any emotional connection. They simply seek to produce parts in volume breaking apart the various job functions so that anyone could perform jobs with minimal training, allowing them to get to work quickly.

Kiichiro Toyoda thought out-of-the-box when he came up with his way of production using just-in-time. It resulted in surpassing the Ford production system. Initially the Toyota Production System was intended to evolve into single-piece production. The Toyota Production System, developed by Kiichiro and Taiichi Ohno, focused on being a system that goes out into the place of work, gathering wisdom where the action is using a tool called gemba (out in the field, at the location, go and observe), and then by integrating and learning from the strengths of different processes. They also came up with the idea of the "multiskilled operator" and made this part of the system. They integrated multifaceted capabilities in collaboration with teammates to perform multiple tasks, instead of executing just one of those small, divided, and dissected job functions. In this interconnected production environment people connectedness becomes stronger and they share wisdom and ingenuity. This brings out a new type of production system that ensures daily improvement practices. Toyota does not permit, in principle, the creation of an assembly line layout revolving around "remote islands" where an operator works alone and where it is impossible to work together as a team with other workstations.

The employees need to adjust themselves to varying workloads. This idea comes from Toyota's thinking habits and emphasizes "human interconnectivity." This reflects back to the image of the fighting Mikawa warriors in battle. Their chance to win increased because they had stronger links among themselves.

No matter whether you choose the Ford or the Toyota system, there are pros and cons to both. However, in today's rapidly changing market, with demands for more variety and specifications of cars, the advantages of the Toyota method are that it emphasizes the holistic features of systems as well as their purposefulness and interconnectedness (links). This has made Toyota able to exert larger market strength as an application of systemic thinking, which is also a paradigm of Breakthrough Thinking.

THE IMPORTANCE OF A PROCESS-FOCUSED MANAGEMENT

In an interview by the *Nihon Keizai Shimbun* and the *British Financial Times*, Akio Toyoda, the president of Toyota Motor, emphasized that one of the biggest risks for business management is when they rely on target values or key performance indicators (KPIs). He said, "An organization may lose control when management is based on numerical targets such as units or dollars because everything other than those targets becomes invisible." He also said, "It is advantageous for those close to the actual operation of a business to control their operation focused on specific goals, but management should not follow that practice."

Post–WWII Japan focused on studying Western styles of business management. These became diffused throughout Japan and merit-based business administration systems were showing an overwhelming influence. This is result-focused business management, also considered a form of carrot-and-stick business execution. Advanced computer performance increased its diffusion to various parts of our world wrapped around the buzzword of management by objective (MBO). Not only in business but also in academia do we see a focus on the idea that students of today are obsessed with data collection, information, and numbers. This includes everything from the entrance exams before getting into college and all the way to chasing targets at work. This is an unfortunate but harsh fact of our current environment. Management employees are required by stockholders to achieve results. Management, in turn, places targets on their employees in order to achieve the results they need. Lower-level employees are then subjected to carrot-and-stick management. This can result in employee misconduct when they are pushed too far by their targets, which are sometimes window-dressed as "challenges." Employees can make any number look good, even if it means using backhanded techniques. For example, Enron, Volkswagen, and others have distorted their public data and have become victims of the distorted pursuits of a results-oriented business administration. "Business management by results" is based on the theory X of management advocated by Douglas McGregor, who believed in his hypothesis about humans that they can only be motivated by using "carrots and sticks."

Toyota's thinking habits are closer to theory Y in which they believe people can be happy at work. This thinking habit is a succession of thinking habits of the Mikawa-Tokugawa warriors and Ninomiya Sontoku who believed in diligent work. At Toyota it is often said that "results follow hard work," and before Toyota knew it, its employees' diligent efforts made Toyota a superior top performer. Diligent hard work is extremely critical. For example, in the development of the Toyota Production System multiskilled operators worked hard and magnified all their creative juices to develop all the pieces of their just-in-time production system. They would experiment, test theories, and apply their ingenuity both as teams and autonomously. Everyone was equipped with the same thinking engines, as shared by their leadership, and then they ran their own engines. A thinking engine is defined as a person who can think and work by himself. You can find thinking engines integrated into each working cell, where they work autonomously in Toyota's version of the assembly line. The entire work environment becomes obsessed with searching for solutions. They behave as if addicted. Employees work hard and are happy. They are not motivated by carrots and sticks. The result was that Toyota's Kaizen involved everyone in a furor of activity.

Is the reader aware of the difference between European fast trains and the Japanese counterpart called *Shinkansen* (bullet train)? The first vehicle of a European train is the locomotive. It has big engines designed to pull a large number of cars. We draw a parallel between this approach and a company led by one autocratic president. However, Japanese Shinkansen train cars are each equipped with motors and these motors work together to achieve more power. These trains have the ability to run at high velocities, running over 300 km per hour. We parallel this with Toyota's thinking habits. Toyota uses a typical Shinkansen model, since those who became involved with the process are instilled with "thinking engines." These employees become autonomously behaving creative individuals. Toyota, therefore, is a corporation in pursuit of business management focusing on the emphasizing processes, and it differs significantly from other companies in that it utilizes a management-by-results structure. The interesting difference created by using the thinking habits of Toyota can be exemplified by the difference between Japanese and European high-speed trains.

THINKING BROADLY STARTED FROM A SOURCE DOWNSTREAM

Since the early days of Work Design, Breakthrough Thinking has adopted the principle of "upstream processing/downstream processing," which requires us to think about input at its source while exploring the resulting output downstream in order to comprehend the complete big picture. Toyota emphasizes processes in its thinking, but its thinking habits about processes gives us additional insight by tracking back to what is happening upstream while simultaneously expanding our understanding of what is happening downstream.

Take a look at Figure 4.1. It is important not to confine our thinking strictly within the walls of a Toyota plant. Instead, we need to expand our perspective to consider supplied parts (an input), the parts for the parts (input of the input), and the parts for the parts for parts (input of the input of the input). Using this approach, we arrive at the original materials, meaning the source raw materials like oil or iron ore. Also in reverse, we consider what happens to the vehicle that we produce. We look at the car that is to be delivered from a plant as an output, which is than an input into the next level of output, and then to the next level of output, and so on. Eventually you will reach the heart and mind of a customer. Go all the way to the extreme: ultimately, in the end, the car will eventually be dumped and recycled.

Toyota deploys its business as a whole by expanding on this process of evaluating the entire demand chain. This occurs in addition to its emphasis on processes. For instance, Kiichiro founded a steel mill before launching his car assembly business. The "god of car sales," Shotaro Kamiya, founded a company that imported petroleum from Indonesia, which

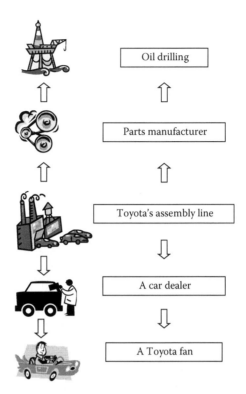

FIGURE 4.1
Thinking habits of a demand chain.

became an indispensable input for his automotive business. The company was called Japan Indonesia Oil and Kamiya became its president. This company is now planting kenaf with the long-range plan of building a new plant in Japan that will use the kenaf leaves as input material in the production of automotive parts.

Downstream Toyota is expanding its network of used car sales outlets. Toyota is focused on becoming a 100% recycling firm by applying environmental considerations throughout the entire demand chain, from upstream to downstream. Also the company seemingly plans to construct a demand chain that will optimize procurement and support its just-in-time practice, again by connecting all elements of the upstream and downstream processes.

Toyota's new supply chain hopes to pull from its customers. It prefers to call it a demand chain. Normally this kind of chain is called a supply chain. However, Toyota is working hard to construct a holistic network system that will function toward connecting all processes as support systems mechanisms and thereby organize a complete pull mechanism that connects all the way from the customer. The goal is that all processes can accommodate a just-in-time practice for the customer. The ideal picture of its demand chain starts with the customer placing an order for a car. This information reaches down to Toyota, which in turn initiates the production of the ordered car and makes all the necessary arrangements for parts and components throughout the entire demand chain.

In recent years, a trend not only in Japan and the United States but also in emerging markets is the recycling business of discarded vehicles. Those "approved shops" that comply with specific standards are provided with relevant technologies. The goal is to utilize recyclable materials in order to realize a sustainable automobile infrastructure with a significantly reduced load to the environment. In particular, eco-cars use rarer earth materials that need to be recycled. One of the many benefits of the improved reuse of precious materials is the lowering of production costs.

BUILDING SYSTEMS STRUCTURES OVERSEAS

Toyota has its own thinking habits that it incorporated into itself and that apply a form of oriental philosophy focused on purposeful, holistic, and interlocking or linking ideas. This was inherited from Ieyasu Tokugawa, the Mikawa warriors, and forefathers of Sakichi and Kiichiro. Now let us see how these thinking habits have been put into practice in Toyota's global marketing efforts.

The beginning of Toyota's full-scale global strategy was triggered by events including when the U.S. legislature created the Corporate Average Fuel Economy (CAFE) standards in 1975, and the second oil crisis in 1979 when the Big Three U.S. automakers experienced poor business performance. These events caused the United States to apply pressure on Japanese automobile imports including Toyota. For example, in the name of self-regulation, the United States imposed a constraint on imported units and required more U.S.-made parts and component content in the vehicles. Toyota felt a need for a breakthrough at that time. American manufacturers found themselves behind in the race and they started to seek additional countermeasures. The NUMMI project between Toyota and GM was triggered by these restrictions. It became the first-ever joint-venture enterprise triggered by these events.

During the startup period of this joint venture, the majority of the supplied parts came from Japan. In Japan, NUMMI was given the nickname of the "gaichu" or outsourcing project, since about 70% of original cost content of the vehicles produced by NUMMI came from Japanese supplied parts. This was the first time Japanese buyers placed orders with U.S. manufacturers, which made it challenging and confusing for the purchasing staff as they confronted the culture of American business. It was common practice in Japan to hold numerous conversations and discussions with a vendor before finalizing the parts specifications. They concentrated on using the vendor's experience and working together to design-in the end part. On the other hand, American suppliers were more independent and offered only their conventional, standard products. They declined any suggestion to discuss their designs or share their manufacturing processes. Because of a fear of being charged with collusion, and wanting to avoid breaching antitrust laws, the Americans permitted the Japanese to talk and work with only their account executives. This included price negotiation. Toyota insisted that it had no intention of collusion but wanted a focused discussion about the manufacturing process in order to optimize quality. Toyota made a series of presentations hoping to convince the Americans that they were simply trying to incorporate Toyota's practice of building quality into the process. Consequently, the American counterparts understood the Toyota approach. The result was that Toyota and its American vendors achieved a deeper relationship and were able to work closely together with a special focus centered on the quality engineers. In the end, cost reduction was achieved and it became possible to get consistent and stable parts sourcing from the vendors.

The NUMMI joint venture also adopted the Japanese practice of policy deployment, in which a conference was held for the senior management of their suppliers at the beginning of each new year in order to brief them on NUMMI's annual policy. This occasion was also used to check the vendor's progress by project and to modify their activities if needed. The Big Three U.S. automakers, being afraid of prosecution by the antitrust laws and because of the difference in business culture, had not held these types of meetings with their parts suppliers. However, use of the concept of design-in where parts suppliers take part in the design of the product early on, was slowly becoming adopted among American suppliers. Consequently, GM was able to develop several smaller cars with improved mileage. This resulted in an increase of their sales market. Toyota benefited because of its ability to double its parts sales and that became the mutual benefit of this win–win relationship. This became an excellent benchmark example of how Toyota's broader global marketing program would work.

BUILDING THE STRUCTURE FOR THE NUMMI LAUNCH

Prior to the launch of production at NUMMI, Toyota examined the conventional decision-making system utilizing tandem management authorization, which both sides initially thought would be necessary for GM and Toyota to work together. They determined that it would take too much time to work through the hierarchy each time a change decision needed to be made. Instead it was decided to set up a committee for a lead-time reduction project consisting of vice presidents from various respective production fields of expertise. The focus of the integrated effort was to increase the decision-making speed concerning process and parts changes. They chose a parallel decision-making system where the committee could make quick decisions about particular products (Figure 4.2). This committee studied the production process and parts challenges throughout the product line. For example, a focus was placed on how to achieve parts commonality between the Toyota Corolla models and the Chevy Nova. They wanted to set up systems that would lower the costs of the parts and shorten the overall delivery lead time.

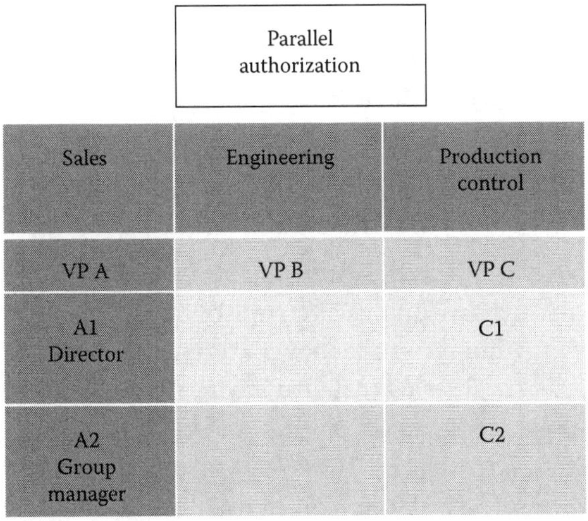

Parallel authorization		
Sales	Engineering	Production control
VP A	VP B	VP C
A1 Director		C1
A2 Group manager		C2

FIGURE 4.2
Parallel authorization.

For instance, in one particular study of parts for the Nova, the committee defined a goal that would ensure achieving the planned launch date. This occurred through parallel authorizations under the authority of the vice presidents of both the engineering and purchasing departments respectively.

Consequently, the lead time for launching a new vehicle into production at NUMMI was significantly reduced. It took just 2 years for large components such as exhaust gas–related systems, large-dimension molding components, or heat exchange units to be created.

The signing of the joint production memorandum of understanding between the two companies occurred in June 1983. The start of the new entity was in February 1984 and the first production of vehicles took place in December 1984.

Even though NUMMI met numerous complaints and concerns raised by the traditional divisions of GM as well as from several U.S. parts manufacturers, NUMMI enjoyed the benefit of large volume purchasing agreements for Toyota parts. GM benefitted by being able to reduce the average weight of its own cars. Both sides were winners. In those days the U.S.-mandated CAFE legislations specified that a manufacturer producing cars with an average weight of over 1500 c.c. was required to pay a penalty per car assembled. GM wanted to avoid that payment. CAFE took effect in 1979. Its purpose was to promote fuel economy while curtailing gas-guzzling cars.

BUILDING SYSTEMS ARCHITECTURE FOR LOCAL PROCUREMENT

The NUMMI project was Toyota's first large-scale production facility outside of Japan. It required that a large volume of parts needed to be procured in the United States. Toyota, of course, organized a powerful team to investigate the feasibility of locally purchasing performance-determining critical components such as engines and transmissions. However, in the end Toyota decided to initially source those parts and components from Japan. A joint team was created that included engineering, quality, and procurement. They engaged in an in-depth study and identified parts that could be procured locally, like seats, glass, tires, battery, audio equipment, bumpers, lights, and die-casted parts (plastics, aluminum, and others). The target was to achieve 50% local content by the end of 1984 by purchasing from U.S. manufacturers, thereby allowing them to launch vehicle production.

As NUMMI's results became visible, they were pressured to accelerate the launch date, but they were facing challenges with local parts procurement organizations where suppliers failed in their delivery commitments. Unfortunately, these failures were treated as accepted and as matter of fact. This delay acceptance occurred because the initially assumed lead time for the original launch was now shorter. Additionally, NUMMI learned that Toyota's engineering department in Japan could not release their drawings as required. Toyota had no mechanism for supervising its suppliers' drawings while working together with those suppliers. Building and maintaining an internationally acceptable system that provided suppliers with technical information became a large task. As an example, Toyota had to create a system in which the auto assembler clearly indicates its requirements for a particular part, for its volume, delivery date, and how testing should be conducted for a prototype, and all this had to be done in English. Additionally, Toyota offered its assistance to those same parts manufacturers for improved development and evaluation while simultaneously supervising them.

In order to secure an improved level of quality for locally procured parts, engineers from Toyota and GM worked with the engineering staff of the local suppliers where they applied a design-in concept to involve stakeholders in designing more efficient systems. As a result of these systems, the Nova automobile produced by NUMMI was welcomed into the marketplace for its outstanding quality and it was first in customer satisfaction for the U.S. market.

In addition to that, Toyota also created the following systems:

1. Opened the NUMMI Detroit Office as a part of a system to provide technical and quality information for parts manufacturers
2. Integrated their research and development (R&D) function into North America by setting up operations in Ann Arbor, Michigan, following the design-in approach
3. Setting up a "Design Promotion Committee" within Toyota in order to support American suppliers who were challenged with overcoming the handicaps of language and geography as a part of their corporate commitment
4. Enhanced Fellow Design Engineering Systems (EFDES), a system dedicated to supporting suppliers' own commitment in quality and cost

All these paved the way for Toyota's global marketing strategy in the following years.

EFFECTIVE OUTCOMES OF THE EFFORT OF TOYOTA'S SYSTEM ARCHITECTURE

As a result of Toyota's effort in the 1980s, it became the number 1 "Made in America" car in 2016. A Cars.com assessment that year determined that the Toyota Camry, assembled at plants in Kentucky and Indiana, was the most made-in-the-U.S. car you can buy. "It reinforces the Americanization story of Toyota," says Bill Fay, general manager of Toyota Motor Sales, U.S. "We operate ten plants in the U.S., build more than 2 million vehicles here, and 71% of our sales in America are vehicles built in North America."

Toyota has created millions of jobs, not only for factory workers, but also parts supply chain workers and distributors, marketing people, research and development people, repair and service people, recycle people, and so on. Since the beginning of the NUMMI project Toyota will invest more than $10 billion within 5 years in the future of the United States focused on development for the future.

ESTABLISHING A BASE IN EUROPE

Hoping to achieve the same success in Europe that Toyota achieved in the American market, Toyota applied the same principles that were used in the United States when it introduced local production for its vehicles in Europe. Toyota focused on producing localized models that facilitated an increase in local employment, allowing Toyota to strengthen the local parts sector. This allowed Toyota to contribute national income and GDP growth to the particular country. The direct export of assembled cars from Japan was insufficient to meet this goal and Toyota had to consider how it should help create more jobs, facilitate more parts procurement, and facilitate local economic growth. In North America it increased the credibility of Toyota including its contribution to the local economy, which enabled a well-balanced marketing platform. However, the situation was different for the various European countries and in China. Germany, France, and Sweden, in particular, which had excellent industrial capabilities and the European Union (EU) members, including these three countries, found little appeal in Toyota's approach. These nations enjoyed nontariff benefits and they also had surplus industrial capacity. Toyota's local production in the United Kingdom of both vehicles and engines was well-organized facilitating exports to other EU members in addition to Japan. On the other hand, Toyota's launch in France was not as successful and its market share in the EU marketplace including Germany and Italy still remains low, suggesting it has more challenges to tackle in the coming years.

IDENTIFYING OPPORTUNITIES: THE LAUNCH TO THE REST OF THE WORLD

Growing beyond the United States, the first overseas production of Toyota cars started in countries like Brazil where many Japanese descendants migrated. The first oil crisis of 1973 hit the United States and caused its government to put pressure on Japan requesting a joint collaboration with the United States, the aforementioned NUMMI, joining with GM as its start of full-scale overseas production. Systems technology was transferred as part of this project, such as procurement, production, logistics, and sales. They were all applied as part of the subsequent deployment of Toyota's global strategy, which blossomed as the global expansion of its business. In the United States, for instance, Toyota started the 100% Toyota–owned Toyota Motor Manufacturing, Kentucky, Inc. (TMMK) where it produces such models as the Camry and Avalon. Just a half year later, Toyota Motor Manufacturing Canada started to assemble the Corolla, Matrix, and RAV4. These chronological details are summarized in the Appendix: Global Network of Toyota of this book for future reference. Together with Toyota's expansion of local production, other Toyota group of companies, like Denso and Aisin Seiki, started volume production of parts and components in the 1990s. Toyota and Lexus have received high acclaim in each of their brand images as they compete with Mercedes Benz for the top position in the luxury car market.

Figure 4.3 shows the locations of Toyota production footholds and total production volume as of 2015. (Also see Appendix: Global Network of Toyota.)

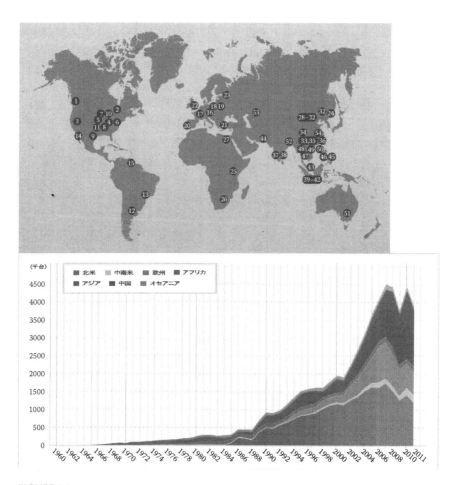

FIGURE 4.3
Global production sites and production volume in years. (From Toyota Global Newsroom.)

SIGNIFICANCE OF NUMMI

The NUMMI project was a major stepping-stone for Toyota in the global marketplace and as a joint venture with GM. It opened a new chapter for Toyota's global marketing. Until then, Toyota had exported cars from Japan, but it was this joint-venture project with GM that triggered Toyota into becoming a full-fledged manufacturer outside Japan. NUMMI ended its activities and now Toyota operates independently in the United States and contributes to the economic development of all the countries where it produces cars. It creates local employment. Toyota simply applied its learning from the NUMMI Toyota–GM joint venture and used this effort to share its original production systems concepts with the world. Figure 4.3 shows Toyota's growth in the world.

OVERSEAS MARKETING WITH EMPHASIS ON QUALITY, COST, AND DELIVERY, AND CHANGES IN VEHICLE SALES

As shown in the marketing strategy of the Nova model, Toyota used its marketing strategy to emphasize QCD in overseas markets, where QCD emphasizes a commitment in quality, cost, and delivery, thereby winning confidence in the Toyota brand. Based on its experience in the American market, Toyota compiled its own manual for standardization where its wisdom was reflected. This allowed the launch and application of systems like PDCA (Plan–Do–Check–Act) focused on acquiring local customers. Because of this, Toyota's brand has been positively recognized throughout the world with its focus on the customer. Figure 4.4 shows Toyota's overseas sales growth. Its overall sales in markets other than Japan have already surpassed domestic sales in Japan, demonstrating the dynamic growth of Toyota as a true global enterprise.

To summarize this chapter, we identify the third secret ingredient used to help explain why Toyota is strong. This requires that we mention that

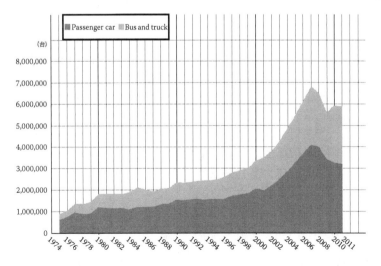

FIGURE 4.4
Shift in overseas sales units.

the company has successfully embodied the concept of systems, stressing "purposeful, holistic, and interlinked" thinking.

TOYOTA'S GLOBAL MARKETING STRATEGY: SECRET INGREDIENT #3

A principle of Breakthrough Thinking—Breakthrough Thinking views the world by declaring that "everything is a system." Breakthrough Thinking adopts a unique view of systems allowing us to comprehend everything as an organic entity. We need to pay attention to its purpose and its position in the holistic big picture of interlocking relations with others. A breakthrough thinker tries to figure out: what is the purpose for its existence, what is the big picture (the high level perspective), and how is this system interrelated or linked with others.

Conventional wisdom—"Everything is a part of system" represents Descartes's mechanistic reductionism theory believing that dividing and analyzing the system can lead to insights. We need to take a materialistic view. Conventional thinking overlooks the reason for a system's existence or its purpose and blinds our eyes to the big picture, forgetting how all the system elements are linked.

At Toyota—Toyota's thinking habits emphasize the konpon (the essence). It considers the total optimization and interconnectedness or linkages. It views everything as an organic system. It sees traditional systems as inherited from previous generations. Toyota has advocated these unique concepts to reflect its belief in systemic Kaizen and integrated systems, and considers the elimination of isolated islands on the assembly line. Toyota tries to visualize the invisible. Visualizing is not the same as seeing because it focuses on comprehending something, as Taiichi Ohno had repeatedly stated. Toyota does not believe in management focusing on results. Rather, it focuses on the process, as seen by the Toyota Production System (TPS).

Question for Reflection

Discuss the essential elements in creating a marketing strategy system.

5

The Hybrid Thinking Engine Drives Toyota: Breakthrough Thinking's Four Principles

Conventional theories of marketing utilize a form of reductionist thinking. This is based on analytical thinking, where we use the analysis of a situation by looking at the past and the present in order to formulate a marketing plan. Using this approach it is believed that the future is seen as an extension of the past and that it is possible to project into the future by studying the past and the present. Unfortunately, if the future deviates even slightly from this extension of the past, this conventional approach suddenly becomes nonsense. Figure 5.1 depicts how our conventional thinking habits are obsolete. We recognize that the prediction methodologies we studied in college are now impractical. Recognizing that there is no future by using an extension of the past is seen not only in the automotive industry but also in other fields. We are in a turbulent age in which traditional marketing theories based on the past and the present are inapplicable. We find more and more examples of the failures of these tools, causing them to become unpopular. In particular, in global marketing it is getting to be more complicated and we see rampant cases of people screaming, "We cannot find the future simply by using an extension of the past." Instead, a new marketing approach that better fits our current turbulent age utilizes Breakthrough Thinking. This method is gaining increased attention. Breakthrough Thinking's thinking habits view everything starting with its essence, and this approach has become an important tool.

FIGURE 5.1
Our future is not an extension of the past.

It has become obvious that conventional approaches for creating marketing strategic plans based on the analysis of the past and the present have become obsolete. Today we are living in the midst of rapid change. We repeatedly hear of failures where analysts are claiming, "We can't see our future by simply using an extension of the past." Accordingly, we need to activate our creativity by utilizing "design thinking," where we ask questions like: What are we really trying to accomplish? What should our goal be? How can we accomplish our goal? We need to go back to the basics. The roots of design thinking does not believe in the future as an extension of the past, but it creates our future using the philosophy of "doing," advocated in the early 1970s by Gerald Nadler and Shozo Hibino, one of the coauthors of this book. Today this approach is getting attention in many parts of the world and is being referred to as design thinking. If we simply move forward into the twenty-first century and pretend that this is an extension of the previous century, the earth would soon become uninhabitable because of massive air pollution. These types of predictions are unacceptable. Humans are moving to design their own future and it does not happen by simply following the past.

We should stop pretending that the future is based on the past and the present. Rather, as the old Sakichi used to say, "We should go back to the essence and basics of everything, seeking the ultimate goal, and take actions in pursuit of these goals." An organic, growing, and changing state is the only option. The authors of this book recognize that Toyota has been influenced, to a large extent, by these types of thinking habits.

BREAKTHROUGH THINKING'S FOUR PRINCIPLES OR THINKING CIRCUITS

Breakthrough Thinking gives us a completely different thinking process, often referred to as a thinking circuit, which is uniquely different from conventional reductionism thinking. We will now compare these two ways of thinking (Figure 5.2).

In conventional marketing theories we are taught to analyze the past and the present in order to create an extension out into the future. This employs a thinking circuit referred to as "analytical thinking." However, in today's tumultuous world where the future is not a simple extension of the past, this thinking method has become invalid. Breakthrough Thinking employs a different thinking circuit focused on design thinking where we start by first asking ourselves the reasons for the existence of the product or service and how it relates to the customer, clarifying the purpose of the product or service, designing its ideal future state,

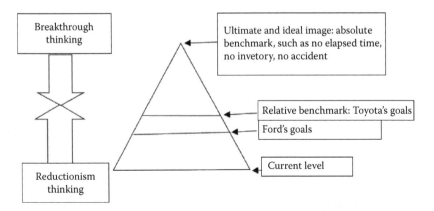

FIGURE 5.2
Image of ideal future solution.

and searching for the best possible solutions in the future design of the product or service. This approach designs a future for the product or service by creating "living" solutions, transforming themselves as the situation surrounding the product or service is continuously changing. Marketing in a turbulent age starts by recognizing this new way of thinking and realizing that it is critical. This understanding occurs only after we recognize that the two ways of thinking are completely different. We start by taking the readers on a journey through this new thinking circuit.

STEP 1: THE PEOPLE INVOLVEMENT PRINCIPLE—PEOPLE ARE AT THE CENTER

Marketing is not necessary if there isn't a customer, if there aren't people involved. A fundamental part of Breakthrough Thinking is placing humans at the core of everything. Who is involved? Who are the stakeholders? Marketing must focus on users and customers as the key central players of the marketing effort. It is not about supplying goods and services. Only through authentic and thorough customer service can organizations remain effective in today's markets. This concept must absolutely be mastered first. Unfortunately, in reductionist thinking, we often make technology, materials, and facts and figures the center of our efforts. Sadly this thinking often overlooks the human faced with problems. In Breakthrough Thinking a problem is defined as "matters that weigh on your mind." Incorporating this broader perspective, we must involve anyone connected with automobiles and automobile services as well as those under their influence. In the case of automotive marketing this includes anyone involved in the prevention and solution of problems associated with the use of automobiles. People are at the source of the data, the information, and the ideas. It is critical to identify who is involved in building, driving, using, supporting, or anyone who is influenced by a particular automotive marketing system, and to let the necessary individuals be involved at the appropriate time. In building a business model for new car development processes, we should remember that only the customers know what they really need. Since the days of Kiichiro, Toyota has sought 100% customer satisfaction.

STEP 2: THE PURPOSE PRINCIPLE—EXPLORING THE REASON FOR EXISTENCE

Our current turbulent age calls for the pursuit of the essence of everything. We should ask what should be, or what is the ideal, or what is the purpose, rather than focusing on data and planning the future as an extension of the past. Traditional reductionist thinking is fact and data centric and is the basis of "truth," whereas in Breakthrough Thinking we adopt a systems philosophy focusing on a holistic systemic view, where "purpose" becomes the focus. Without identifying and focusing on the purpose, a system will disintegrate. In other words, purpose is the basis for a system's value and existence. At the highest level, when a corporation loses its purpose, the value of its existence goes away and it goes bankrupt.

Breakthrough Thinking seeks after the fundamental system. It seeks for the essence of the system, by asking questions like: For what reason does it exit? What is its purpose? What is the purpose of that purpose? It all starts with finding the essential reason for the system's existence. We identify its intrinsic quality as well as its essence. This is also true if the system is focused on the creation of a product. Instead of developing a product with a focus on the imagined superficial needs of customers, we eliminate routine product development by seeking the second-level purpose of the first-level purpose (What is the purpose of this first purpose?) and thereby identify a latent or fundamental purpose. For instance, when a purpose of the automobile is identified as "moving from point A to point B," we realize that we do not need to drive a car at all. Instead we can use a train. This is one of the reasons that the younger generation of today is not as interested in cars as was the previous generation. When asking what is the purpose for moving and expanding the purpose of this previous purpose, our attention shifts to something like "to feel excited." This second-level purpose would encourage us to choose a new car.

More specifically, pursuing the purpose principle requires us to identify the main player(s) in a system and drives us to a different solution. We arrive at the essential purpose and it drives us to a higher-level existential value of a thing, focusing on the main player(s). Recognizing different level purposes causes a change in what we identify as a solution. By looking at higher-level, larger purposes instead of lower-level, smaller ones, our solution space expands enabling us to find a truly optimum solution. Toyota's Japanese catch phrase "Fun to Drive" embodies the company's new product development policy by focusing research efforts on this higher-level purpose. Toyota wants its customers to enjoy driving rather than simply viewing cars as mere means of transportation.

STEP 3: THE FUTURE SOLUTION PRINCIPLE—ULTIMATE THINKING

Traditional reductionist thinking focuses on learning the facts of the past and present. It analyzes previous and current activities. Breakthrough Thinking focuses on learning from the desired future, ultimate, and ideal state of an item. It focuses on the item's ultimate purpose or essential foundation. It is impossible to create new product demand as long as we place our entire focus on an extension of the past. As in the case of the late Steve Jobs, we should exploit a higher level of customer sensitivity. We should gain inspiration from the future and visualize an ideal state. Rather than comparing with competitors or with other excellent companies by using relative benchmarking, we need to envision an ultimate, ideal state by using "absolute benchmarking."

Relative benchmarking is where we compare ourselves with other companies, and using this comparison as we design our plan for the future. The boss often asks questions like "What are our competitors doing?" We are asked to "investigate what other companies are doing and use their example in order to create our own future plan." This approach represents commonsense, conventional reductionist thinking. Whereas when using absolute benchmarking, we focus on an ultimate goal searching for a result that jumps beyond what our competitors are doing. We try to identify a higher-level goal. Breakthrough Thinking encourages creativity using absolute benchmark as the first step, thereby bypassing competitors. For example, instead of trying to reduce cycle time by 30 minutes or reduce inventory stock to a two-day equivalent when compared with Ford Motor, Toyota pursues goals like zero time and zero inventory, as demonstrated with Toyota's focus on just-in-time production. Does this sound absurd? Is it a castle in the sky? No! What these types of goals accomplish is to incite innovation, creativity, efficiency, and effective performance. The previous goal puts a limit on accomplishment and achievement. The new, higher-level goal eliminates lower levels of performance and productiveness as it moves us toward an ultimate state that would otherwise be viewed as impossible and unachievable. It drives us toward solutions that we are otherwise unable to execute. When you copy another's improvements by looking at an extension of the past, it wastes time and increases costs. In the end, the best you will be able to accomplish is to become similar to your competitor. You want to place your efforts toward leapfrogging ahead of your competitors. For example, no matter how much you improve a bicycle, it will never compete with the pleasure of driving a car that is designed with a focus on being fun to drive.

It is important to realize that as we create ultimate and ideal future states or "future solutions," we need to keep many of these future solutions on the shelf for the future. When creating these highly desirable and ideal states that were focused on achieving higher-level purposes as identified by using purpose deployment, they should never be forgotten or ignored. When identifying larger purposes, our range of choices increases and reexamining these choices on a regular basis will orient us toward even more, higher-leveled, purpose deployments.

When you identify an ideal future solution your objective becomes clearer and you become naturally empowered to search for and identify additional improvements and future innovations. Even if they seem currently impossible, such solutions may become feasible in the future and these ideas lead us to revolutionary solutions that may inevitably change the way you live and think. The ideal future solutions principle encourages us to create more options for substantially improved systems solutions by focusing our efforts on a long-term, stretch goal or purpose.

As we seek ideal future solutions, it is useful to apply the principle of regularity. Regularity in this context suggests that we focus on solutions first by considering only "major conditions" and "priorities." This is a very effective tool in creative thinking. There exists an unlimited number of exceptions. However, we need to stay focused on the lower number of primary conditions or high-priority points. Once we have agreement on the primary conditions of the product or service under consideration, we can temporarily avoid dealing with the exceptions. Identify a global future solution first. Then, at a point in the future, we can build up subsystems to deal with the exceptions by following the "living solutions principle" that we will discuss in the next section.

STEP 4: THE LIVING SOLUTIONS PRINCIPLE—SOLUTIONS THAT KEEP CONTINUOUSLY CHANGING

Reductionist thinking does not account for inconsistent behaviors. However, in our current turbulent times, everything is constantly in motion and changing, much like those meandering sheep. Breakthrough Thinking takes this into account by designing ever-changing "living solutions." These solutions allow us to move closer to an ideal state. As we define an ideal, for example zero inventory, this ideal urges us to identify solutions allowing us to satisfy our customers while still maintaining a minimum level of inventory. For example, we could identify a new system that supports a just-in-time inventory management system for a specific group of parts.

The difference between ideal future solutions and living solutions can be explained as follows. Future solutions call for designing an ideal state that achieves a purpose without considering exceptions and unexpected conditions. It also calls for seeking other optional solutions as subsystems to meet those exceptions only after achieving the ideal solution.

You may wonder why we wouldn't start by considering the exceptions first. There is an infinite number of exceptions that would make our solution too complicated. That is why we create universal solutions first, temporarily as a starting point, by employing "prioritize thinking."

LAUNCHING THE "BREAKTHROUGH THINKING ENGINE" GLOBALLY

Ever since its foundation, Toyota has always sought to identify uniqueness using its process for collecting data. It gathers data and information at the actual place (for example at the location where the sale occurs), for the actual subject (automobile sales to customers), and using the approach of a company thinking about design. It uses the approach of focusing on, designing, and constructing systems that take this approach into consideration, as elaborated in the first three chapters of this book. Toyota has used "analytic thinking" in some areas of its corporate activities, but at the same time they have employed a "hybrid thinking engine" in search of solutions always focusing on collecting information with a purpose

(Figure 5.3). Consequently, Toyota has emerged as a global player in automobile business.

In the next chapter and beyond, the authors elaborate about the thinking circuit of Toyota from a perspective of the tool Breakthrough Thinking. They will show how close Toyota's thinking circuit is to what has been incorporated into Breakthrough Thinking.

Chapter 6 deals with Toyota's company philosophy and how it strengthens improved human capabilities. It regards humans as critical resources and its business starts with a focus on the customer as being critical to the process. Chapter 8 deals with ultimate and ideal future solutions. In Chapter 9 we see how Toyota uses a thinking circuit to seek ever-changing and realistic solutions. Toyota's production floor also employs analytical thinking tools in order to activate their hybrid thinking engine moving boldly forward into the world marketplace. Table 5.1 is a summary of the two thinking patterns discussed in this chapter. The authors' goal for this book is for you to understand how Toyota is driven by its hybrid thinking engine. This strong engine is what was used to thrust Toyota in the global marketplace.

The hybrid thinking engine refers to the utilization of dual driving engines just like what we see in Toyota's hybrid cars. This maximizes creativity by taking advantage of each of their respective positive features. When employing conventional reductionism thinking for production floor improvements and data/information collection to achieve our goal, and also taking advantage of the benefits of Breakthrough Thinking for

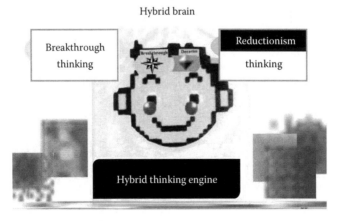

FIGURE 5.3
The hybrid thinking engine.

TABLE 5.1

Toyota's Hybrid Thinking Engine

	Reductionist Thinking	Breakthrough Thinking
Thinking pattern	Analytical thinking	Design thinking
Thinking direction	Generalize	Focus on the specific (Chapter 2)
Information gathering	Extensive information gathering	Only purposeful information collection (Chapter 3)
Epistemology	Fact-centric	Systems-centric (purposeful, interlocking, and holistic) (Chapter 4)
Approach	Analysis	People phase (Chapter 6)
	Find what's wrong	Purpose phase (Chapter 7)
	Replace with solutions	Future solution phase (Chapter 8)
	Embedding	Living solution phase (Chapter 9)

more strategic planning, we receive dual benefits. People at Toyota have turned this into a thinking habit, maximizing creativity by utilizing and integrating different tools as a hybrid that allows them to move themselves ahead in the rest of the world.

Question for Reflection

Discuss how you should use the two thinking engines. How should they be used differently?

6

Secret Ingredient #4: A Company That Nurtures People—The People Involvement Principle

YOU SHOULD RESIGN IF YOU HAVE TO LAY OFF PEOPLE

The warrior Ieyasu Tokugawa was supported by a group of Mikawa warriors. The unity of those Mikawa warriors, supported by the culture and tradition of the Mikawa region, is known to be stubbornly strong even today.

The "Toyoda Platform" written by Kiichiro Toyoda advocates to "always strive to build a warm and friendly homelike atmosphere at work." This emphasizes the virtue of a family-like tradition. Kiichiro Toyoda repeatedly told his employees, "I am obliged as a proprietor to avoid the dismissal of any of my employees." He also said, "My ultimate moral obligation is to prevent personnel cutbacks as much as possible." He even created a memorandum of understanding with Toyota's labor union agreeing to "absolutely have no layoffs." Toyota, right after World War II, was struggling. Its business health was desperate. The banking consortium that supported it demanded that the company practice "personnel cutbacks" causing tension between management and labor to reach a peak, leading to a large-scale labor strike. Toyoda decided to step down because the company was forced to have a layoff and he never came back to Toyota. Since this challenging experience, the management of Toyota transformed its policy to harmonize with its labor union and has focused its business operations toward an emphasis on humanity. This thinking habit has now been incorporated into "The Toyota Way 2001" and it is been shared by Toyota in every location throughout the world.

THE SECRET TO TOYOTA'S PERSONNEL EVALUATIONS

As Japan lost confidence in its conventional business practices, such as its once-popular system of career-long employment, its practice of seniority-based wages was also reexamined. Toyota was seeing more cases of unproductive work practices. Other companies had scenes where employees did not trust one another or their company as companies adopted merit systems as part of their personnel evaluation. This phenomenon, one that Kiichiro Toyoda disliked, is widespread throughout today's Japan. In spite of this trend, Toyota's thinking habit has been kept intact as a Toyota way.

Toyota, as seen by the Toyota Production System, seems to believe that processes and systems trigger behaviors and therefore results. This includes its personnel assessment system. Believing that human capabilities would transform themselves as a result of the system, Toyota rejected any values-based assessment. However, it tries to hone humans and develop individual growth. In a different example, Nissan Motors underwent a revolutionary transformation under Carlos Gosun, its new chief executive officer, who brought in a new set of thinking habits in an attempt to motivate each individual by imposing individual targets. He assembled commitments for compulsory short- and medium-term targets that were shown to shareholders. This thinking habit of Nissan under Gosun and the one of Toyota are contrasting examples. Many business organizations are emulating the example of Nissan but Toyota has retained its thinking habits.

In operations, Toyota has been practicing management by objective, whereas its senior management supports a different way of thinking. According to Toyota documents, managers are assessed based on the following parameters:

1. Creative solutions—Demonstrate the ability for outstanding planning. At the organizational level, this means identifying the quality aspects of everything. This is interpreted as the ability to identify the essence of everything. It calls for identifying breakthrough ideas free from the barriers of tradition. It searches for freedom from an obsession with power as well as superb planning based on a long-term perspective. It means the company wants Breakthrough Thinking in its organization, seeking for the essence by looking for the purpose and

the ideal state followed by identifying and creating working solutions out of those ideal future perspectives.

2. Task execution—The ability to move an organization forward and to obtain results by facilitating and motivating people. Toyota wants the ability to move forward by seeing the essence, presenting ideal future solutions, motivating people toward those solutions, creating systems that drive appropriate motivation, and making appropriate decisions that will move the organization in the desired direction. For managers, the word *facilitate* means "to make a process or system easier." The ability to execute tasks means that the manager has the power to execute a hard assignment even when it calls for Breakthrough Thinking. Its progress needs to constantly be checked.

3. Organizational management—The ability to organize the "collective geniuses" of all the employees and to create teams that will optimize the performance of the organization. Resources should be focused on building a system of operations where the existing structure may be challenged. For instance, this book's author Koichiro Noguchi exercised this ability in a preproduction startup at New United Motor Manufacturing Inc. (NUMMI) where he organized "management teams for major new parts startup" focused on breakthrough innovations throughout the organization.

4. Use of people—The ability to nurture employees' capabilities and the abilities of team members. This includes offering periodic and scheduled guidance and training in order to bring out their best performance. This is a typical application of Toyota's thinking habits involving personnel assessment. As a company it stresses making people not cars.

5. Personal magnetism—It calls for an ability for the manager to be trusted and to invigorate the people around him or her. Noguchi realized the importance of creating confidence and trust from those who worked with him in the overseas operations sites. It took work, but after some effort he successfully increased his credibility and the people he worked with appealed to his magnetism.

These management assessment criteria clearly confirm that Toyota views employees as an asset and not as a cost. Toyota tries to enhance their value. In this style of management there is no room for "management by results," as in the case of merit-based appraisal systems. Instead, Toyota emphasizes the capabilities of the people who create products as well as the network of their relationships. Its inherent thinking habit focused on "making of things starts with making of humans" is ingrained in today's Toyota and is taken from the approaches of Ieyasu Tokugawa, Sakichi Toyoda, and Kiichiro Toyoda, and it has manifested itself in Toyota's personnel management structure.

In *Profit Beyond Measure*, H. Thomas Johnson writes, "management by mechanical results (a management by reductionism thinking) is shattering relationship links within many corporations, causing long term organizational collapse. Toyota, with the adoption of a management style emphasizing the development of networks of relationships (also known as management by Breakthrough Thinking) keeps growing in performance." In an attempt to simplify this approach the authors found the business management perspectives (thinking habits) of Ford and GM as a dramatic contrast with Toyota's management focus and thinking habits. The shift in thinking described by Shozo Hibino and the late G. Nadler in their book *Breakthrough Thinking* (1990) is taking the place of traditional thinking in business management today.

THINKING HABITS FOR PEOPLE DEVELOPMENT

Fujio Cho, who served as president of Toyota Motor, expressed the following during a newspaper interview:

> Making things starts with making humans. This statement embodies the natural born spirit behind the making of things and I believe that the making of people occurs by instilling this spirit into people through the types of tasks we assign them. The spirit of making of things changes the mind into a respect for the production environment, respect for those who work there, respect for the principles behind the actual location of what is happening, attempts to learn from failures, constantly challenging everything, searching for improvement after improvement, and so on just to name a few of the cultural shifts that occur. This spirit or cultural shift (thinking habit transformation) is not only critical for everyone working there (direct and indirect), but also for management within any manufacturing environment. Toyota Motor, from its foundation as well as during the days of old Sakichi Toyoda, has used this approach (thinking habit) and has achieved its growth by building capacity through these methods. The most critical point for Toyota was in transforming younger generations within Toyota

and its group of corporations to adopt and inherit this way of thinking. The goal was that in the long run the established expertise and knowhow would be inherited by the younger generation while at the same time expecting them to comprehend and succeed in developing the spirit of the making of things. However, what is critical for a business enterprise is keeping its people growing and developing proper systems and organizational structure. The business must focus on how to provide a growth enabling environment. In order to accomplish this, I am convinced that we must emphasize training, where people acquire the tools for creative thinking (thinking habit), and develop the values and culture through repeated use of these tools. This is not dependent upon the level of education alone, but it introduces employees to something they were previously not aware of.

Continuing in the thoughts of ex-president Cho, "Toyota's further expansion calls for growing people, especially the succession of Toyota's thinking habits which have been inherited and shared over many generations." Showing respect for Taizo Ishida of Toyota, the late Konosuke Matsushita, founder of Panasonic, stressed, "Matsushita Electric doesn't produce consumer electronics. It develops humans." This became his personal business management philosophy.

By inheriting the thinking habit of making people, Toyota has witnessed significant benefits in the versatility of its personnel. Its culture now has the ability to provide more creative, thinking employees in the various fields of its endeavors.

A secret of growing human capability within Toyota lies in its "hands-on approach to encourage its people to challenge everything, including systems and issues in order to create solutions for optimal results."

THINKING HABITS OF ASSEMBLED ASSOCIATES

Hibino, one of the authors of this book, had numerous interactions with Toyota and its affiliate companies and he was always impressed by them. All the employees were quiet but cheerful and hardworking. Additionally, the thinking habits were evident everywhere as they searched for solutions. They worked together and interacted as teams. He found this same culture at Aisin Seiki and at the Toyota auto parts affiliates.

Over the years, Toyota has applied its thinking habits to identify problems, to identify solutions, and to implement these solutions autonomously using informal groups called *jishu ken* (independent study groups). This differed significantly from the "quality control (QC) circles" that became a social phenomenon in Japan and later around the world. QC circles are autonomous but were considered to be an extension of the employees' jobs and were practiced regularly as a formal activity that was incorporated into the corporate structure. When previously informal activity becomes formalized, manualized, and made compulsory, employees rapidly sacrifice their imagination and creativity. Change becomes difficult and employees feel discouraged. The faithful implementation of any job instruction manual is often called for. But it must be treated as a standard that is reduced to the most simplistic level, thereby allowing for the feasibility of adjusting this standard to satisfy individual requirements so that everyone can execute the job. This explains why the old QC campaign has lost its appeal and TQC has become known as *totemo qrushii* circles (extremely torturing circles). On the other hand, Toyota's informal groups are not meant for complying with the lowest level of achievement by following manuals; rather, it is focused on pursuing the highest level of systems solutions in a lively and exciting way.

We can learn some valuable lessons from both QC circles and jishu ken by looking closely at their thinking habits. Hideharu Kaneda, formerly an employee at a Toyota affiliate, mentioned in his book *Hyper Toyota-Style Change Leadership*:

> While QC Circles are activities employing reductionist thinking, Jishu-ken gives us the opportunity for deduction (Breakthrough Thinking). In QC Circles, they learn the methodology of quality control using groups allowing them to apply practical problem solving techniques in on factory floor. However, Jishu-ken implants ideal state thinking and facilitates an overwhelming victory when it is implemented.

It is a conviction, not a theory. This makes all employees realize that what they feel is not wrong. Identifying problems is a positive activity. Searching for and comparing actual problems in their current state with the ideal state is a constructive activity. Consider your own corporation or enterprise. Are your QC circles only employing conventional thinking? Toyota organizes employees together with a focus on their new thinking habit in order to expose failures and to apply improvements one at a time. The authors of this book would also like you to discover the answer to the question of why Toyota is strong, and realize that the answer lies in its unique thinking habits.

Successful thinking habits originating from the days of the Mikawa warriors apply wisdom and ingenuity and never stop searching for planning solutions. Toyota employees remind us of the success of the Mikawa warriors. They work not by following a strict set of instructions, but because they enjoying their work. The result is that they focus on a solution-holistic approach.

TOYOTA'S LABOR–MANAGEMENT RELATIONSHIP

Labor–management relations at Toyota are strongly influenced by the company's thinking habits. This is an extension of the old Edo period. The structure of the relationship was built upon the Toyoda Platform written by Kiichiro Toyoda when Toyota Motors was founded. Toyota's labor-management relationship relies heavily on the concept that the entire organization is one big family. This is shown in his document that states "by exemplifying a fraternity spirit, we should establish a family-style culture." This thinking habit is identical with the one from the Mikawa warriors in the Tokugawa era and it is also similar to the beliefs of Nichiren Buddhism. It is also consistent with the philosophies and thoughts found in Sontoku Ninomiya's "Ho-Toku-Kyo," a belief that when you do good you get rewarded. When Toyota was on the brink of bankruptcy, Kiichiro tried to keep his promise of employment security but in the end was unable to live up to this commitment and was forced to resign from his presidency. Subsequently their family-values were denied and a modified "thinking habit" had to be introduced, which could have included concepts like communism, liberalism, individualism and other values from outside Japan. Relations between labor and management became confrontational and intensive labor disputes occurred. After what turned out to be a bitter experience, Toyota's labor and management alike began their return to the original thinking habits of the Mikawa warriors. Management started to assemble employees who helped each other like the Mikawa warriors did and attempted to remove the conflict. They created a large number of informal associations like *Hoyokai* (association of individuals with similar training), *Hoseikai* (association of high school graduates), *Hoshinkai* (association of college graduates), and others in an attempt to encourage dialogue between labor and management. Consequently they reached an agreement and signed the following declaration:

1. We will contribute to the development of our national economy through the growth of the automobile industry.
2. Our labor–management relations will be based on mutual trust.
3. We will pursue the increased prosperity of the company as well as maintain and improve working conditions through increased productivity.

Sharing these basic principles, Toyota's labor and management became one team. They worked together and created higher quality, lower cost, and developed a system of mass production.

Later, in 1996, Toyota's labor and management declared their "focus on the twenty-first century" as follows, in order to keep progressing toward becoming a global enterprise:

1. We, as a global corporation, will contribute to the development of global economies as well as building a global community.
2. Our labor–management relationship shall be based on mutual trust and accountability.
3. We will stand on common ground and play our respective roles toward building a better business environment where people can work vibrantly in the creation of increased value-added products.
4. We will strive to become an affluent society by improving the living standard for the employees with our eyes focused on Japan as a whole.

Through these statements Toyota's labor and management pledged to work together toward the overall success of the company.

When considering these declarations, we saw the same solidarity among the Mikawa warriors. They also reflect the thinking habits and spirit of Sakichi and Kiichiro Toyoda. The labor–management relation is a product of Toyota's thinking habits originating from the past.

STRONG SOLIDARITY

There are numerous explanations for why the Mikawa warriors had a strong sense of solidarity. One explanation takes a geopolitical perspective looking at the Mikawa region. In comparison with other affluent regions such as Kanto, which includes Tokyo; Kansai, which includes Osaka and Nagoya; and Enshu, which is a harsher place to live and which is often described as the "cold and dry wind of Enshu," Mikawa is surrounded by mountains and is a challenging place to inhabit. The harsh living conditions influenced the thinking habits of the people who lived there. Most of them worked in agriculture and the farming environment was harsh. To sustain their hard-to-produce crops, the solidarity of the farmers was considered to be indispensable.

The Mikawa warriors, including Ieyasu Tokugawa, were farming families who grew up in these harsh conditions. They had to be united in order to defend themselves from invading neighbors. Toyota Motor was born out of this environment. Today, those municipalities, like the cities of Toyota, Kariya, Anjo, and others where Toyota and its affiliates work intensively, are known as Toyota's castle towns. But they all used to be a large farming zone, referred to as the Denmark of Japan. Thinking habits encountered in this region can be summarized using the following words: "work and achieve prosperity together, localism (for farming and area development), a pioneering and a progressive spirit." Although today's Toyota is a global player, the company used to concentrate all of its major plants in this region until the 1980s. Naturally the majority of its employees came from farming families and their solidarity was stronger than what could be found in rival companies. It is essential to remember that those Toyota people who came from these farming zones have a strong unity for today's Toyota and its affiliates.

In addition to internal unity, Toyota maintains a strong bond with its affiliates and suppliers, more so than any of its competitors do, and this approach dates way back. Toyota organized associations such as *Kyohokai* (for parts suppliers), *Seihokai* (for the manufactures of jigs, dies, and gauges), and *Eihokai* (for plant construction, facility, and work). Toyota Motor regards those member companies as its family members and encourages the use of their thinking habits to produce cars using the one-team approach. Accordingly, their bond of solidarity is extremely strong, and Toyota has offered its technical assistance and quality-control expertise to those lower-tier industries in order to facilitate their "design in," "joint development," and "joint production" methodologies. Those suppliers have in turn organized their own joint improvement study groups.

The 1997 case of Aisin Seiki's fire was a good example of this solidarity and how it attempted to prove its effectiveness. At one of the older plants of

Aisin, water was sprayed on magnesium powder in error, causing a spark, which turned into a fire and soon the entire wood plant was on fire. Valve production of 30,000 per day was halted. Toyota's own assembly had to be halted because of the chain reaction on the just-in-time system's supply chain. Then something astonishing occurred. Kyohokai members, including Denso, as well as second- and third-tier suppliers, worked together to initiate alternative methods of production of these valves using temporary process lines. Although the fire was expected to disrupt Toyota production for at least a week, Toyota's car assembly was able to be resumed in just 3 days. This episode demonstrates the strength of their unity.

Another quote from the book written by Shoichiro Toyoda is

> An approach to place humans at the center, an approach to instill new blood into the management systems, and to share their wisdom for management practices, has been inherited, uninterrupted by utilizing the mutual efforts of both our labor and management. They have a strong bond with sales agents, contractors, and the labor union. All these are at the heart of Toyota's competencies and are built on the sweat and hard work of our predecessors.

UNITY IN COMPANIES

The successful solidarity of the Mikawa warriors' unity may collapse someday because of the law of entropy if Toyota's thinking habits become weaker over time and through increased globalization. This book warns us of this possible danger. An example can be seen in the case of the failure of Sharp Corporation as depicted in the published article "Shaapu Houraku" (Failure of Sharp) by Nikkei. Here is a quote from that article:

> Sharp's tragedy took place after its internal power struggle. They made a bad decision which required an unrealistic and large investment into liquid crystal display business units for its Sakai Plant in Osaka. After it started to fail a management crisis occurred which provoked intensive infighting. This distracted the organization from exerting an appropriate amount of effort toward identifying effective solutions and the damage cascaded uncontrollably. ... Previously Sharp Corporation was one of the excellent companies with a credo based on sound and steady business practices. It demonstrated its uniqueness prior to hitting this crisis with the failed

business of LCDs. Mechanical pencils are still referred to in Japan as Sharp pencils, invented by its founder Tokuji Hayakawa. Starting as a small business, Sharp was soon able to introduce many "first in the world" products. Its business environment was centered on family-values. Its engineers could work in a free and creative atmosphere, which they stressed was like working in heaven. … This article describes how a famed enterprise could suddenly fail because of an internal power struggle.

It was true that Sharp Corporation was one of the most innovative companies. It offered a series of groundbreaking products such as LCD applications for television receivers, refrigerators, air purifiers, solar batteries, and more. The company also adopted a family-like business management environment similar to Toyota. This once-excellent company failed because individual employees struggled and worked against each other, which resulted in employees losing jobs. Sadly this is a part of human nature. Toyota cannot be the exception. This family-based culture needs to exist in more companies.

Toyota underwent restructuring in 2016 by adopting an integrated company structure with a total of seven companies consisting of four that were grouped by vehicle type (compact, passenger cars, commercial vehicles, and luxury vehicles) and three more grouped by engineering and components. The purpose of this new company system was threefold: (1) getting ready for 10 million units of production volume, (2) reorganizing the business units that had become too large into business units by function, and (3) nurturing a new breed of potential presidential candidates. The last one, as it often the case, may lead to power struggles, which may trigger organizational collapse. Accordingly, it calls for Toyota to come up with a creative way to prevent the potential power game while still sustaining its solidarity, which it inherited from the Mikawa warriors.

THE POWER STRUGGLE IN NOMINATING A COMPENSATION COMMITTEE

The result of a recent revision of Japan's Commercial Code is that we are seeing an increased number of companies launching nomination and compensation committees. The changed law was designed to increase corporate governance and it is functioning as intended, but the new clause is simply an imitation of the one in the United States and it has raised numerous issues when considering the "uniqueness principle." Here are just a few examples:

- Decreased morale—Conventional personnel systems of many Japanese corporations including Toyota Motor find it acceptable to see a person who started in a rank-and-file position to have a goal of being promoted higher, even achieving the executive level including president. However, the new rule allows external individuals to be brought into positions like board members. The concern is that this would lead to lower morale within the enterprise.
- External board members decide critical matters—Author Hibino once got involved in a retailing business where more authority was given to external board members and they exploited their power causing an internal coup d'état and a power struggle. Other companies have also shown internal confusion by playing the power game. If this happens at Toyota, its strong unity from its legacy of the Mikawa warriors might be lost.
- Against the principle of uniqueness—Installing a nomination and compensation committee calls for a minimum of two external board members. This is a concern in Japan. It is difficult to find capable officers to supervise businesses from the outside, as they have less liquidity in the high end of the labor market when compared to a similar market for such business executives in America. What happens if an external executive, without knowing Toyota's hybrid thinking habits, turns Toyota into an ordinary big enterprise by making decisions using generalized American business practices? This may cause bankruptcy even for Toyota.

THE START OF PRODUCTION IN THE UNITED STATES

Following the second oil crisis in 1979, each of the Big Three automakers in the United States experienced a deterioration of business performance results. They urged for pressure to be placed on Japan, limiting its car exports. This resulted in Toyota studying the option of creating a full-fledged automotive production facility on the U.S. mainland. The result was the start of the NUMMI project as a joint venture with GM. One of the first challenges was for Toyota to apply its concept of "Toyota makes humans, not cars" in the context of this new and different culture.

As Toyota announced its draft plans to set up a new plant in the United States, many state governments tried to invite Toyota to their home states. They discussed pros and cons for attracting Toyota, such as transportation, labor quality, supplier availability (just showing a list of names), and financial incentives as positive inducements, while also listing negative factors such as coal mining, the strong influence of the United Automobile Workers (UAW), and frequent floods. Toyota set up a commission to study the options from the various candidate states. They meticulously checked geography for a plant location, local population for employees, transportation infrastructure, port access, and even the chance of flooding or earthquakes. In many cases, proposed locations were on fields or farming land, and these local people had no experience working in larger production environments. Toyota identified leaders by the relevant functions and created an all-Toyota team with a focus on procurement and experience working with other departments. This team was not just ad hoc but also considered elements of a lasting system focused on organizing big projects. The team was made up of a group of professionals. For team selection Toyota chose people from Toyota Japan as well as those who had experience with GM and Ford. Also experience with other local suppliers in the United States was considered. They learned different thinking habits from different backgrounds. The first result of this integrated project team was the creation of the subcompact fuel economy car called the Nova.

For supervisors, GM asked for volunteers who would temporarily transfer to work on this project. Toyota named and requested specific individuals within its organization to come to NUMMI. It had to be extremely complicated for them to be transferred from Toyota to this facility. Back then GM was still the global top performer in the world and considered itself to be the best. Machine operators were recruited by NUMMI from the local population.

After recruitment, everyone underwent twofold training. One set of training focused on providing education about how to launch a new plant focused on the volume production of cars in collaboration with a designated mother plant in Japan. The other training focused on developing the capacity to develop leaders. The mother plant was Toyota's Takaoka facility where everything required hands-on education. The preparation including training in facilities and personnel for learning everything from how to reduce the inventory of materials, parts, and assembled cars, to tools like 5S housekeeping practices following the practical approach of the genchi-genbutsu (actual place, actual item) principle. The Americans also learned how to make improvements by attending Kaizen meetings for their relevant sections. They followed the approach that the training of staff occurred after operating hours and without compensation. That was the rule when applying Toyota's jishu-ken style.

For this kind of training, it is standard practice for the Japanese side to cover the cost. However, in this case, it was astonishing to see that the local state government was very cooperative in sharing the costs for the training in Japan, as it realized that this training was a great opportunity to enhance the quality of the local workforce by having them learn how Toyota builds cars in Japan.

HOW THEY OVERCAME CULTURAL CONFLICTS

Whenever we do business in different countries, we often encounter a situation where common practice fails to get results because of the unique country differences in the areas of culture, custom, and tradition. This was something that was always accepted as ordinary in Toyota and not expected to receive special consideration. Japan received unexpected reactions from Americans. Toyota regards its employees as family members, in compliance with the "Toyoda Platform" that calls for a "display of fraternity spirit and encourages a strong family culture." Accordingly, back in Japan, the employees would offer their honest impressions, just like the ancient Mikawa warriors. However, American management and employees have been masters and slaves historically and the employees have been subject to their masters. The masters ruled and the slaves were forced to work. That explains why strong labor unions are organized in the United States resulting from confrontations between management and labor with frequent and intense struggles. In the late 1980s when Toyota went to the United States, the UAW had faced a decline in its membership. It was increasingly becoming inactive and was being criticized for its existence. Its value as a trade union was being challenged. Toyota started the launch of its new plant under these circumstances.

A handful of Americans with experience at the Fremont Plant of GM, the forerunner of NUMMI, offered advice in private and in informal locations like bars to tell Toyota how typical American workers would attempt to sabotage production. They described the American worker as lazy. They sarcastically offered the following examples of the bad habits of the American workers that have occurred over the years:

- When suppliers failed to deliver parts, workers receiving the parts would be delighted. When the delay was announced by microphone, they cheered, shouting for joy and dancing. For these employees, thinking about how to overcome such delays was secondary.
- A daily event was for them to drink beer or other alcoholic beverages during working hours.
- They often left a scratch on an assembled car body intentionally so that they could get overtime rework after the production line stopped. They enjoyed this and referred to it as "going to the hospital."
- They do not pay attention to the speed of the conveyor and work slowly in order to get extra income and overtime.
- Any line stoppage caused by missing parts would be welcomed by American workers with a cheer.

All these reports of how American workers think sounded surprisingly different from the thinking and behavior of the Toyota workers in Japan. They discovered a large difference between the behaviors and the thought processes when they compared management, laborers, and parts suppliers. They found minimal commitment from all the stakeholders when it came to improving the process and building better cars. The Toyota people had assumed a more positive relationship would exist.

Toyota, in those days, was compared to the Tokugawa clan. Toyota was a small, unfamiliar fly and the workers from the gigantic GM conglomerate did not want to listen to any recommendations from the Japanese side of the NUMMI partnership, no matter how often the Japanese asked what is it they are trying to become. Because the GM employees had been trained to work just as their manual says, and their job was physical, they saw little requirement for management thinking or creativity.

Little by little Toyota started to instill the Japanese way of doing things. It brought a different management style focused on mutual growth for all workers. It adopted systems to create and enhance heart-to-heart communications, similar to what existed among the old Mikawa warriors, by introducing the practices that were common in Japan. Examples include managers eating lunch at the same place as the workers; all employees singing karaoke songs together; managers and employees playing sports during off-duty hours, going out for picnics, and other group activities. NUMMI displayed big banners of "Good Thinking Means Good Products" throughout the inside of the plant and promoted Kaizen action campaigns so that the workers would discover the joy of creative thinking. Additionally, the company displayed and shared performance results using numerical values. This led employees to realize that sabotaging would be disadvantageous to themselves. More people started to think seriously about their work and found it more rewarding. Eventually the bad practices declined.

The people involvement principle found in Breakthrough Thinking produced a positive effect by encouraging all relevant stakeholders, such as UAW officials, management, supervisors, and workers, to be engaged in the process and to let employees realize their role in all stages of the organization, including capital investment and the setting of standard production times.

FACED WITH STRONG RESISTANCE

Following is another example of the cultural friction that occurred. While GM and Toyota competed to prove who was better, the workers of GM had no understanding that their employer was getting old and declining. Roger Smith, then chairman of board at GM, was afraid of disclosing the weakening of the company even though it was obvious when considering the signs. The two big car assemblers fought each other over how the work should be distributed during the launch stage of NUMMI. Middle management of GM was particularly confident about their approach since they believed GM was the best company in the world. They did not respond to requests aimed at following how their partner does it. Then Smith realized that GM could not compete in the production of subcompact and fuel-efficient cars. He sent a message to the supervisory staff of GM to put a halt to their process methodologies. Instead they were to watch how Toyota organizes its production facility and use it. This message put an end to the turmoil among GMers. Unfortunately, it demonstrates the typical cultural friction that occurs when deploying marketing strategy plans within different cultures.

TOYOTA'S GLOBAL MARKETING STRATEGY: SECRET INGREDIENT #4

A principle of Breakthrough Thinking—Information lies in the heads of people as well as at the location of the job. Collect the wisdom of the people in order to create collective genius. Enlightenment produces personal transformation. Engage and involve people at all stages and allow them to be enlightened.

Conventional wisdom—Experts can solve everything. Consult with them and work covertly. Only experts can define and create all solutions. Managers are expected to be experts.

At Toyota—Toyota values the actual job location. People at the job site organize jishu-ken by themselves in order to concentrate on problem solving. Creativeness and wisdom at the job site are more valuable than experts. An informal group of solution-aholic team members can show destructive power.

$$\text{Toyota's Profit} = \text{Consumer's Price} - \text{Cost} + \text{VE Effect}$$

Question for Reflection

The people phase is said to be the most critical in a marketing strategy. Discuss why this is so important.

7

Secret Ingredient #5: Explore the Reason for Existence— The Purpose Principle

EXPLORE THE REASON FOR EXISTENCE: A BACK TO BASICS APPROACH

In order to have "thinking habits that are free from copy-catting," it is critical to establish a thinking habit that approaches everything starting with its essence and with the basics. Kiichiro Toyoda worked diligently to solve each of the fundamental management challenges that he encountered in launching an automobile industry in Japan. He utilized his fundamental principles rather than adopting Western systems. Ford Motor, which preceded Toyota, used a conveyor belt system. For the ordinary entrepreneur there would have been no doubt that they should imitate the Ford system in developing their own conveyor belt system. But the thinking habits of Toyoda were different. He focused on the question: What was the purpose of using the conveyor belt system? He tried to go back to the basics and sought answers. He found the answer to be "seamless flow." He thought a seamless production system required a "just-in-time" approach as the ultimate tool. Toyoda's thinking habits caused him to seek the essence by going back to the basics. This brought him to the completely new concept of just-in-time, something Ford did not discover. Ford Motor applied the conveyor belt system in its search for volume production but missed the idea of the essential purpose of the conveyor belt.

The "three-stage rifle shooting," employed by the coalition forces of Oda and Tokuagawa in the battle of Nagashino and discussed in an earlier chapter, was created after searching for the essence behind shooting a gun. This changed the tactics of how to use a gun. The forces faced the rushing cavalry of the Takeda army and found their guns could be employed more effectively by laying an ongoing barrage of gun fire, a gun fire curtain, rather than just shooting at an approaching individual enemy. The result was spectacular. It was a victory of the Oda–Tokugawa alliance that redefined the purpose and use of rifles. Kiichiro Toyoda, similarly, changed the definition of the purpose of the conveyor belt into one of "transporting parts on a just-in-time basis" instead of the Ford use of conveyor belts that "moved parts in quantity." He changed how to assemble cars by grasping the essence of the process.

SAKICHI TOYODA DIALOGUES WITH THE TOYOTA CENTRAL RESEARCH AND DEVELOPMENT LABS

Following is another anecdote of Sakichi Toyoda, the father of Kiichiro Toyada. He motivated and encouraged the research and development group by saying, "We should seek for research and creativity that will allow us to jump ahead of the time." This thinking habit of Sakichi should give the reader pause. First, it refers to research and creativity. The traditional meaning of *research* usually focuses on discovering a scientific truth and researching means to write a dissertation. However, Sakichi stressed that research and development (R&D) needs to realize that the "final goal of an invention is its complete and practical use. You should not put your invention into the marketplace unless you field-test it completely." Sakichi was innovative in thinking an invention can achieve its purpose only after it has found commercial usage.

This book's author Shozo Hibino was invited by Toyota's Central R&D Laboratory to help it adopt Breakthrough Thinking. The conversation at the time was interesting from a perspective of Sakichi Toyoda. Toyota Central Labs was using a form of "pipeline pushing" in those days when planning its workload. Pipeline pushing is a technique where results are generated by blowing or pushing work through a pipe. Using this technique, the labs were blowing hard on one end of the pipe, using an abundant budget, and hoping that would increase a speed of the output created by the lab. However, the results had been disappointing. Their creative productivity had fallen so low that the success rate had fallen to 3 out of 1,000 or even 3 out of 10,000. Even though the labs kept blowing hard on the pipe, hard enough to generate 10,000 options of promising technologies, they only had 3 successful commercial applications. The reason of this extremely poor performance was simple. Pipeline pushing promoted a conventional way of thinking where they analyzed, created, and then verified their ideas. This practice successfully generated multiple "technological seeds." Those seeds are validated to ensure their marketplace appeal. Unfortunately, since in the past researchers were motivated to create reports and ideas using the conventional approach, they blew out a long list of ideas rather than focusing on how to create products that had marketability. Consequently, the labs generated a pile of paper, which satisfied the pipeline pushing approach, rather than following the spirit of Sakichi Toyoda. Faced with these consequence, the top officers of Toyota Central Labs finally decided to return to the basics of Sakichi Toyoda, who said that the "final purpose of an invention is to make it practical," and that "you should not put a product into the marketplace unless you have tested its commercial relevance."

The labs decided to focus on Breakthrough Thinking in order to enable the creation of concepts with a focus on the consumer looking at their essence and values. By changing its approach in the R&D department, focusing on creating useful products by integrating technologies and information began to materialize throughout Toyota. Toyota realized that it is more critical to market useful products and services that are created as a result of involving the customer, rather than pursuing "truths" generated by data and information. This was a case example of rediscovering the old traditional thinking habits of Sakichi Toyoda at Toyota Central Labs.

THE PURPOSE OF THE 5 WHYS

Taiichi Ohno used to walk the factory floor challenging his subordinates to identify a fundamental root cause behind a problem by using the practice of asking why five times. For example, let's pretend that one of your employees, Mr. A, is absent from work today without notice. You can apply Ohno's technique as follows by asking: Why is he absent without notice today? The answer could be: Because you reprimanded him hard yesterday. The second level question could be: Why did you reprimand him? Answer: Because his work attitude was bad. Third question: Why was his work attitude bad? Answer: Because he drank too much and stayed out till midnight on the previous day and he had a rough night. Fourth question:

Why did he feel he had a rough night? Answer: Because he lost all hope in his life. Question: Why did he lose hope in his life? Answer: He felt his workplace wasn't offering him a good future. Eventually, through this line of questioning, you realize the essential issue is that the company became insignificant to him and his growth. The problem was not his absence without notice. By repeatedly asking why more than five times we get to the root of the problem. Then we can better understand his situation and we can better identify a solution for his absenteeism rather than reprimanding him. The goal should always be to "create a better workplace where each worker can paint for themselves a better future." This demonstrates Toyota's practice of using thinking habits to discover essential issues or root causes, then separate them from the more visible issue, like the employee's absence without notice. This is accomplished by using and repeating the 5 Whys as the tool to solve a problem.

FROM PURPOSE TO THE REASON FOR EXISTENCE

A pursuit of the essence or root cause is possible by using a two-step methodology. The first step is to seek the true root cause by repeatedly asking the question why. The second step is to ask questions about the object's purpose by using the purpose expansion discussed earlier in this book. Both Sakichi Toyoda and Kiichiro Toyoda provided the critical thought process that was needed. Accordingly, they were able to think through and identify the specific purposes. Automobile engineers are normally focused only on the production of cars, but Kiichiro's thought process was different. As he stated, his purpose was "not the assembly of cars but rather to promote the automobile industry throughout Japan." That was his focus as he searched for the essence of his endeavor. His thought process and his insights were extremely unique for business development in his day.

We will now expand our explanation of the purpose principle. This can be a tool to help us identify the essence of the object that we are focusing on. We start on the workshop floor and look at the "functional deployment" (purpose deployment). This is where we introduced "work design" using Breakthrough Thinking. It is where we identify the true function or purpose of the activity (system) that we are engaged in by repeatedly asking the question, What is the purpose of it? This is similar to the root cause tool that we discussed earlier of asking why five times, but instead of drilling down to find the root cause of a problem, this time we are climbing upward looking for the purpose or reason behind doing what we are doing. For example, let's look at the ballpoint pen. Its primary function (purpose) is to write. The purpose of writing is to display a character. The purpose of displaying the character is to display information. The purpose of displaying information is to transfer information. Transferring information is to develop knowledge, and its purpose in turn is to get knowledge, followed by the purpose of creating knowledge. In the end, using the purpose expansion tool, we learn that the true purpose of a ballpoint pen is not to write but to create new knowledge.

As demonstrated earlier, Kiichiro found the essential meaning or purpose of conveyor belts by repeatedly asking what is the purpose. He mentally performed a purpose expansion for the conveyor belt by moving upward toward the purpose of the conveyor belt rather than down toward the root cause. In his mind he performed a purpose expansion. In the case of the conveyor belt, its purpose expansion could go through the following steps. The purpose of the conveyor belt is to move materials, whose purpose is to feed materials along a production line, whose purpose is to manufacture parts, whose purpose is to feed parts seamlessly to production, whose purpose is to assemble parts, whose purpose is to assemble cars (as the customer needs them), whose purpose is to deliver cars to the customer (according to the needs of customers), whose purpose is to deliver a means of transportation to a customer, whose purpose is to deliver freedom of transportation to a customer, and so on. Kiichiro felt that he had discovered a problem with the Ford Motor approach. He was able to redefine the function of conveyor belts: conveyor belts are not meant for the assembly of parts in large volume; they are a tool for the delivery of parts when needed and only in the quantity needed. This resulted in the creation of the just-in-time systems approach.

To most of the readers of this book, purpose deployment may sound unfamiliar, especially when we are requesting the reader to repeatedly keep asking for the purpose of a purpose. However, according to the authors' research, leading-edge thinkers for the essence of any activity or system by identifying the true essence or reason for a system's existence by repeatedly asking for the purpose of a purpose. This often occurs without formally thinking about what they are doing. A consequence of the two civil war–era leaders Nobunaga Oda and Ieyasu Tokugawa was that they won the decisive battle by identifying the essential purpose for firearms, which they claimed was to lay a curtain of fire rather than to aim at a specific individual. This essential purpose, as in most cases, could have been reached almost unconsciously.

There are two ways to take a fundamental approach of looking at everything. One is to repeatedly ask the question why, thereby defining the cause. Those issues that tend to be a search to identify and solve a specific problem, such as identifying the reason for quality defects, would come out of this approach. This is what Ohno did at Toyota. Using this approach has us repeatedly asking the question why until we identify the root cause. The other fundamental approach is to use the purpose expansion method where we identify the essence of a thing, like a system or a process, by asking repeatedly what its purpose is, like: "What is the purpose of the conveyor belt?" and then repeatedly asking for the next level purpose, and then for the next layer of the purpose, and so on as Kiichiro did when he came up with a new way of production.

The first approach has been integrated comprehensively into Toyota's thinking habits by Taiichi Ohno. The latter approach was inherited as an additional thinking habit from the Tokugawa era and was inherited into the first generation of the Toyoda family, including Sakichi Toyoda and Kiichiro. We call these two thinking habits a hybrid of thinking habits, together focused on getting us closer to an essence. The secret of Toyota's strength can be attributed to this hybrid of thinking habits, using them to completely identify the essence of things.

Purpose is the essence that will show us the reason for our existence.

JUMPING DIRECTLY TO THE REASON FOR EXISTENCE (ESSENCE)

Let's discuss another benefit of these thinking habits by going back to the essence of what we are looking at. The goal is to bypass and leapfrog to a position of being more advanced in both enterprises and countries. Conventional thinking suggests that we should learn from those enterprises that are the most advanced and emulate them. This requires research, data collection, and information assimilation, which require time and resources for a study. The more you try to learn from the advanced enterprises, the more your business will be restricted by its business approach, and you will limit yourself and potentially become unable to think creatively. In the meantime, those advanced corporations continue to move forward, while the copiers spend all their time trying to catch up. They restrict and limit themselves from ever being able to take a leadership position.

Kiichiro Toyoda, the founder of Toyota Motor, visited Ford Motor where Ford explained that the purpose of the conveyor belt was to feed parts in large quantities into the production process in order to assemble more cars. However, Toyoda questioned this approach and in his mind identified that its real purpose should be to feed parts just-in-time. That focus, along with a collection of additional ideas, prompted the eventual creation of what we know today as the Toyota Production System. This has been created and has resulted in the subsequent phenomenal growth of Toyota. For them, and for the reader, a decisive point must be whether it is important to focus on the essence as well as the meaning of the system, as with our example with the conveyor belt system that has its existence shifted by redefining it and thereby overturning conventional wisdom.

We are living in very turbulent age. Competition is intense. We can only leapfrog our competition by focusing on thinking habits that bring us back to the essence of whatever is consuming our attention. And we need to do it quickly.

People from developing countries are discovering the power of this thinking habit. They are starting to learn the power of Breakthrough Thinking. The emergence of this new thinking paradigm focused on radical, leapfrog change, as exemplified in Toyota, has brought with it an enormous turning point in assisting developing countries. Traditionally the way they have received official assistance was by treating them as beggars. These countries have been deprived of utilizing their thinking habits because they became increasingly dependent. They were offered dependency-generating financial support. Asian countries have a proverb that states "Don't give away fish as a handout. Instead, teach them how to fish." By giving them fish (Western solutions or money), they are still unable to catch fish on their own. This results in them asking for more fish and increasing their dependency rather than helping them to creatively think and act on their own. Creating this dependency may favorably position the developed countries. This may allow them to exert control over the developing economies of the underdeveloped economies. Dependency makes the underdeveloped countries less capable of thinking creatively because they feel the need to imitate the developed economies, which means they can never leapfrog ahead. Developed countries can maintain control of developing countries by using economic sanctions when those countries get creative and do not toe the line. They need to stay behind and follow the direction of the richer countries and not get too creative.

The current concept of assistance focused on controlling developing nations is just an extension of what was traditionally colonial rule. The only difference is that the mechanism for control is economical. And it is about time to depart from that. Hibino has been an instructor at several of Japan's training institutions that focus on developing countries, such as the Japan International Cooperation Agency (JICA) and the Overseas Human Resources and Industrial Development Association (HIDA). His job over the years has been to teach them how to catch fish. Those trainees are learning Breakthrough Thinking. They were trained to think in a fundamental way and to get them motivated to leapfrog the more advanced countries and corporations. This is similar to how Toyota Motor succeeded in bypassing the automotive industry giants like GM and Ford by creatively thinking from the ground up. Developing nations desire to have this happen for them as well. Developing countries are eager to learn how to accomplish this, but the developed countries might find the results unpleasant.

The reason for a system's existence, or its essence, is different from the god-thinking, god-willing approach of epistemology, which suggests that there is one and only one right way, and the developed countries have already learned that right way.

THE BIGGEST WASTE: RESULTS THAT DON'T FIT THE PURPOSE

Toyota defines waste in production as "activities or events which create results that do not add value." They are constantly searching for opportunities to eliminate the following seven types of wastes:

1. Waste by overproduction
2. Waste by waiting
3. Waste by transportation
4. Waste in processing

5. Waste by holding inventory
6. Waste in unnecessary motions
7. Waste by producing defectives

In order to eliminate those kinds of wastes, it is first necessary to make the wastes visible. Accordingly, Toyota has been promoting a process called "managing by making waste visible." This is accomplished using systems tools that visualize the wastes such as 5S, kanban, and andon. Before we discuss these tools, it is critical that we define waste. An essential part of the Toyota definition is that waste "does not increase added value." This definition requires a second definition. What is meant by added value? According to *Kojien*, Japan's most authoritative dictionary, it is defined as "a value newly created within a business enterprise." None of the wastes listed earlier satisfy the definition of value added, including making more product than is needed to satisfy customer demand, waiting, transporting, unnecessary processing steps, holding inventory, or unnecessary movement. Instead it calls for a new set of thinking habits in order to understand why and how we should eliminate overproduction, waiting, transporting, unnecessary processing, keeping uncommitted inventory, or unnecessary movement.

The authors need to add an eighth waste of "nonpurpose-oriented results." Breakthrough Thinking refers to this as the third kind of error. An example of this could be found in a company that tried to adopt the Toyota Production System. In an attempt to be faithful to the system, the company tried to eliminate its inventory. They asked themselves, "Why should we eliminate our inventory?" followed by, "What is the purpose of this purpose?" and so on in order to continue to seek the essence of the purposes. Using this process they started to see their goal as keeping all their inventory using a just-in-time approach. Accordingly, they discovered that their purpose would not be fulfilled unless they maintained their inventory. Their new approach resulted in them maintaining their inventory. This story tells us that something previously considered not to be a waste actually ended up being a different kind of waste. It became a waste of nonpurpose-oriented results.

MARKETING IN AMERICA

Achieving a result that does not fit to a purpose turns out to be the largest kind of waste. This book's author Koichiro Noguchi avoided this in his

NUMMI (New United Motor Manufacturing Inc.) marketing efforts by asking the question, For what purpose do Americans drive cars? Then he adjusted and adopted his marketing strategy to make it appropriate for Americans.

The American lifestyle is diversified. A large number of people enjoy outdoor activities that involve travel, like picnics and outdoor sports. Their purpose for driving is not simply for transportation but to enjoy the experience of driving. Their purpose can be found in a series of purpose expansions that start with their enjoyment of moving. Its purpose is to enjoy the car's performance. Then, the purpose is to enjoy car styling. Next the purpose is to enjoy living with and owning cars. This is followed by the purpose of having a happy life with cars. And the purpose of that is to enjoy being happy.

Witnessing American life by being on location at NUMMI, Noguchi found that a car is a part of life for Americans and that they appreciate and enjoy living with cars. Accordingly, focusing on the existential value of cars and how they contribute to enjoying life, Noguchi tried to enhance the value of Toyota cars for Americans by searching for and seeking their ultimate goals, as Kiichiro Toyoda stressed when he suggested we look for both the "benchmark of purpose accomplishment" and simultaneously identifying the "target values," as follows:

1. Customer satisfaction is No. 1—Toyoda aimed at the ultimate state of management by objective using a market survey focused on identifying customer needs and which incorporated a merchandising plan based on the PDCA cycle. He validated the customer's level of satisfaction utilizing several surveys.
2. Air pollution control—He focused on the ultimate ideal state that eliminates all pollutant emissions.
3. Scarcity of resource and fuel economy—He developed improved gasoline-free car engines such as hydrogen fuel cell cars and electric cars.
4. Safety and accident free—In addition to more stringent traffic regulations and improved roads, he put more emphasis on connected (communication between) cars and the development of autonomous driving vehicles (artificial intelligence-assisted vehicle control).
5. More family orientation—He focused on trying to become better neighbors. He organized a series of social events, including picnics, dinner parties, and sporting events, which promoted a team spirit.

In all of these campaigns, Noguchi tried to motivate each employee with a specific, nonbinding target that focused on individual needs instead of motivating them by metrics, like measuring their throughput. With these types of goals, he tried to design and build specific systems utilizing a benefits matrix composed of country, department, and the individual. All of this became the focus of deploying an effective marketing strategy.

PAY ATTENTION TO PARTS PROCUREMENT

The NUMMI project had an extremely high ratio of purchased parts cost to total vehicle cost. Therefore parts procurement became a critical task in terms of quality, cost, and delivery. NUMMI had a large number of parts and components that were supplied from Japan without inspection. Management attention was focused on the quality, cost, and delivery of locally purchased parts. Accordingly, the NUMMI team, inspired by Toyota, created a system that would realize our goals while paying meticulous attention to the following six points:

1. Corporate citizen—Pursuing the role of being a good corporate citizen, we tried to nurture and enhance local suppliers.
2. Profitability—With these intermediate goals defined, we tried to incorporate our sales targets with a focus on profitability. Profitability comes from volume sales, not from increased margins.
3. Fair business practices—We paid attention to fair competition by using an open-door policy where our intermediate goals called for the practice of no unfair product dumping as well as our enforcement of a no dumping policy. In order to manage unpaid cost, we applied VE and VA (value engineering and value analysis) as a compensation practice within Toyota. Price is determined by consumers, so when we discussed and decided upon our price we incorporated a consideration of the contribution of VA/VE in both the medium and the long term.
4. Set up VA and VE goals—With a principle focus on local production and local consumption, a car assembler should determine the price of the vehicle as a combination of the current competitive price and the VE target value.

5. Goals—Goal achievement should be reflected in our market share.

6. Setup of incentive and payback bonus—Our payback was to increase based on an increase in purchased quantity.

NUMMI and its suppliers worked very hard together to establish corporate trust relationships. Finally, we gained mutual trust through this prosperity.

In this book we have observed the strength of Toyota from many angles. The conclusion for this chapter, therefore, has to be that Toyota's thinking habits, which focus on seeking out the essence completely, is the fifth secret ingredient of the Toyota methodology.

TOYOTA'S GLOBAL MARKETING STRATEGY: SECRET INGREDIENT #5

A principle of Breakthrough Thinking. The management-level officer should strive to find the essence of the system or process. Ask for a purpose's purpose, in several layers, in order to enlarge our perspective. Choose the largest level of purpose for what it is that you are trying to understand.

Breakthrough Thinking focuses on systems philosophy and purpose.

Conventional wisdom. Working-level personnel should analyze and seek root causes in the problems they are addressing. They should pay special attention to materials and systems by employing reductionism (reductionist thinking) where we find truth (root causes) and past issues along with present concerns, and then replace them with new solutions. This approach is effective for current, short-term improvements but has the flaw of being unable sustain a long-term solution into the future.

In reductionism or fact-centric thinking, fact is the reason for existence.

At Toyota. Toyota is implanted with thinking habits that consider everything's fundamental essence. Repeatedly asking the question why for five or more cycles is how Toyota focuses on identifying the fundamental reasons for a problem. This points them at the root cause of a problem. They also seek for the essential purpose and reason for the existence of a process or system by repeatedly asking questions like what is the purpose of a process or system. This puts structure behind Toyota's hybrid thinking habit. All of this came at a decisive moment when Kiichiro Toyoda identified that the fundamental purpose of the conveyor belt was to feed parts in a just-in-time manner. This triggered Toyota's production system innovation and the result was that it became more competitive than Ford, which maintained a higher level of inventory within its processes.

Questions for Reflection

Discuss why in today's tumultuous age we should plan our marketing strategy from the bottom up in order to create a workable strategy. Describe what "essence" means by comparing an epistemological approach against Breakthrough Thinking and the Toyota approaches.

8

Secret Ingredient #6: In Pursuit of the Ultimate Solution—The Future Solution Principle

THE SECRET OF TOYOTA'S STRENGTH: ULTIMATE THINKING

Toyota's thinking habits have incorporated a thinking habit referred to as "ultimate thinking." The Toyota Production System was developed by using this concept of ultimate thinking. Kiichiro Toyoda said to his subordinates, "Manufacturing's ideal state is not just to have just-in-time inventory using kanbans, but to ultimately have no inventory." Previously we discussed that just-in-time was a valuable stepping stone. It was used to produce what was needed, at the time it was needed, and in the quantity that it was needed. This is a form of ultimate thinking in that it calls for absolutely no inventory at any time. Commonly accepted within Ford's production system was the concept of volume production with large inventories. By averaging setup time across large batch runs, the cost per part is minimized. For Toyota his words sounded offbeat. According to the official book titled *Toyota Motor's 50-Year History*, Taiichi Ohno, who was Toyoda's subordinate, found a 1954 article in a business publication that said American supermarkets are stockless and used just-in-time replenishment. It was just a small article in the paper, but it triggered Ohno to start his own study to help him understand how supermarkets worked. From this he came up with the idea of the kanban system, where the concept of a customer going up to the cashier with their shopping items and money was similarly applied to the factory employee going to get parts using a kanban sheet. This kanban is equal to the money. This concept became the heart of the Toyota Production System and triggered a series of process innovations that ended up becoming the foundation of today's Toyota. It was a victorious moment for the integration of Toyota's thinking habits with the concept of ultimate thinking. If Toyota had the Ford model as its goal, then the kanban system would have never been developed and Toyota would be a different company than it is today.

Kiichiro Toyoda imbedded this thinking habit into everything. For example, he advocated a formula that he borrowed from Ford:

$$Profit = Selling\ price - Cost$$

He believed that maximizing profit ultimately required reducing cost to zero. He explained this approach by using the thinking habit of "wringing out a wet towel," thereby lowering the cost, step by step, ultimately to zero. Toyota has been known to propose an increase in the selling price of its U.S. vehicles in an attempt to save the ailing American carmakers from their pending doom. By applying the aforementioned formula, this proposal would give Toyota, Ford, and GM record profits. However, this would force consumers to purchase more expensive car models. This proposal would only offer short-term relief, like an adrenaline shot; it was not a long-term sustainable solution because ultimately the inefficiency of the American automobile makers needed to be overhauled. Increased price adjustments would only facilitate the American addiction to inefficiency.

Another example of ultimate thinking by Ohno can be seen in his famous practice of a single-digit minute exchange of die (SMED) system. SMED focuses on the drastic reduction of preparation time, changeover, and setup times during production when we are changing from one model or part number to another. Whenever there is a change in production, changeover steps are needed. The thinking habit of Ohno, as the originator of this practice, was ideal and critical to successful just-in-time performance. For example, he required that the changeover time for a certain process that used to take 3 hours in most companies be reduced to just 3 minutes within Toyota. His people, faced with this challenge, experimented with numerous approaches and finally came up with a system for changeover that achieved the 3-minute goal. From this came the story of Toyota's single-digit minute changeovers.

The ultimate and ideal condition in this example was to achieve zero minutes. After his team succeeded in achieving a changeover time of 3 minutes, Ohno asked his people to face the new and more aggressive challenge of creating a system to complete the changeover work instantaneously (in 0 minutes). We need to pay attention to how Ohno's thinking habits shifted from what was initially 3 hours, then down to 30 minutes, then reduced to 3 minutes, then 2 minutes, 1 minute, and last of all the ultimate goal of 0 minutes. He used an ever-changing thinking habit of continuously improving his goal. Toyota currently produces several models of cars on the same production line, and its changeover time is zero, under perfect conditions.

The strength of Toyota comes from an ever-changing series of improvement goals, not by one simple improvement step. Its continuous improvement process is the result of its ultimate thinking.

WHAT DOES "ABSOLUTE BENCHMARKING" MEAN?

Many companies decide their target performance levels by referring to examples of what other companies are doing. However, this method of benchmarking is doomed to failure. It is often replaced by another kind of thinking habit that stresses thoughts like "If it takes 3 days at Ford, we should do it in 2 days." This thinking is based on comparison with others and called "relative benchmarking." Many corporations employ this way of thinking. It motivates people, but it also is an example of saying, "That company works hard. Let's work harder." Even Toyota has used relative benchmarking at the working or staff levels. This thinking habit has drawbacks such as a higher requirement of time and budget and a predisposition to imitate, and it is more challenging to identify breakthrough opportunities. Particularly in today's rapidly changing world, it is more likely to cause a timing error, or the error of the fourth kind in Breakthrough Thinking. For the twenty-first century's fast-changing world, this is becoming an obsolete thinking habit. Just recently a Korean company contacted the author Shozo Hibino requesting information about a client. Presumably, it was a benchmarking survey of the type described here. But using this data, the best the company can ever do is catch up, not leapfrog ahead.

As we discussed earlier, in the case of just-in-time and single-minute exchange of dye (or single-minute changeover), the ideal target should be expressed as "zero cost," "zero defect," "zero time," "zero accident," "zero space," "customer delight," "100 percent utilization," and other similar goals. These standards are absolute values, either in the form of 0 or 100 percent and are called "absolute benchmarks."

The creation of this absolute benchmark does not require data or information collection, or an analysis of cost content. It stimulates one's creativity and draws out the possibility of a creative breakthrough. This is what it takes in order to achieve the top position. Toyota uses absolute benchmarking as its thinking habit. Thanks to this thinking habit, Toyota has been able to creatively produce originality in its thinking which has gained international attention and acceptance. The car assembler is now focused on the development of vehicles with "zero accidents." Toyota is focusing its thinking on the statement, "Don't look for reasons why it won't work. Don't focus on failure. Put your creativity towards how the goal can be achieved." This is the type of thinking that is supporting Toyota's creativity today.

WHAT DOES "ULTIMATE THINKING" MEAN?

Let us review and summarize the theory of ultimate thinking by Toyota. Both Kiichiro Toyoda and Taiichi Ohno utilized the ultimate thinking habit from the beginning.

In 1963, the late Gerald Nadler, coauthor with Hibino, published the book *Breakthrough Thinking* (1990) and came to Japan to share his vision, which at that time was called "work design," in a 6-month workshop at Waseda University's then Institute of Production Studies. At that time, Toyota was constructing its Toyota Production System and took the opportunity to learn work design, which became the theoretical background for Toyota's ultimate thinking model. It became fused into Toyota's overall thinking habits.

Back in those days, work design utilized the deductive method of thinking as it approached issues from an ideal state. The conventional thinking approach emphasized research-analysis problem solving and was called the induction method. After Hibino became involved with Nadler, work design evolved to include a philosophy and approach thereby expanding the theory, and it was renamed Breakthrough Thinking, which is the approach used today focusing on the essence of a process or a system.

Toyota is unique and has demonstrated excellent performance results in the world because it takes advantage of the two different thinking paradigms: reductionism and Breakthrough Thinking. Today, Toyota is exploring global market opportunities, taking on the role of a pioneer for hybrid vehicles, which allow two driving modes: the gasoline engine and the electric motor. This initiative is easier to understand when we comprehend Toyota's focus on the hybrid thinking engine.

Consider the meaning of Toyota's ultimate thinking from a perspective of Breakthrough Thinking. In Figure 8.1 we see the image of a triangle pointing to the ideal future solution using Breakthrough Thinking. This was developed out of the work design approach originating in the 1960s. At that time, it was called the triangle of ideal systems. The vertical axis shows the direction of change, while the horizontal axis displays cost and time. The bottom of the diagram is the current state, and the ultimate or ideal state is shown at the apex on top. The apex, as the ideal state, is the extreme situation with zero cost, zero time, zero space, 100 percent customer satisfaction, and 100 percent plant utilization.

Toyoda wanted his just-in-time system to be at the apex of this triangle and sought to achieve zero changeover time and zero inventory. Ohno worked toward this goal by creating his single-digit minute changeover time and driving it further toward the goal of zero changeover time. This ultimate and ideal state is called the "want-to" state in Toyota. "Want-to" represents one's wishes. Wishing is important as a motivator of people, but

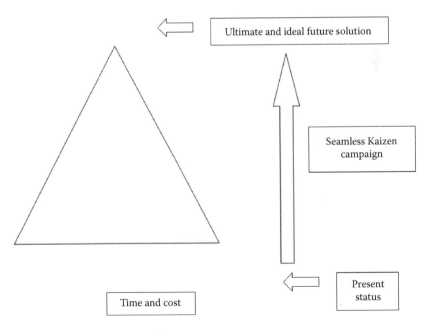

FIGURE 8.1
Triangle of ideal future solution.

there is the concern that a wish might not drive us to the essence. After all, finding the essence is critical when faced with fundamental questions, such as what is the essence or what should the essence be, as we seek for ideal future solutions based on this essence.

Hideharu Kaneda, who once led the innovations team at Kanto Auto Works, an affiliate of Toyota Motor, had studied the work design (Breakthrough Thinking) methodology and wrote the book Choȉ„toyotashiki chienji riȉ„daȉ„ : Kawaritsuzukeru saikyoȉ„ no keiei (or Toyota-shiki saikyō no keiei : naze Toyota wa kawaritsuzukeru no ka). In it he states:

> I was challenged to launch the assembly of a new type of vehicle with zero additional workers during the start-up. Everyone in the plant told me it would be absolutely impossible. However, the result surprised me. We successfully achieved this goal and required zero additional personnel during the start-up period. This effort surprisingly allowed the new model production startup to be much smoother and problem-free. ... While other companies are trying to solve their problems and identify solutions to creative challenges using the inductive method (reductionistic thinking), Toyota is applying the deductive method (Breakthrough Thinking) for its money-making programs. ... Kaizens (change or improvement activities) have traditionally used the inductive method (reductionist thinking). More innovative kaizens have applied the deductive method (Breakthrough Thinking). Kaizens that are focused strictly on what is happening today (short term) should rely on the inductive method (reduction thinking) while innovation focused on preparing an organization for tomorrow should be done using the deductive method (Breakthrough Thinking).

Kaneda preached the importance of using the thinking habits of Breakthrough Thinking. His remarks clearly show that Toyota's thinking habit has incorporated the capabilities of Breakthrough Thinking.

THE PROCESS OF SEEING THE HIDDEN PROBLEMS

"The Toyota Way 2001" is a compilation of the "Toyoda Platform," which represents the structure for Toyota's global thinking habit. The new doctrine presented in the platform consists of two pillars:

- Human ingenuity and continuous improvement
- Respect for all of humanity

In a nutshell, it calls for never-ending improvement by making invisible problems visible (visualization process) while gathering human wisdom and at the same time being respectful of the human capability to innovate and create (to think). "The Toyota Way 2001" formula has become a reality through the application of Toyota's ultimate thinking habit.

Normal business practice is that organizations would start by analyzing the present situation in order to identify defects. Then they would move forward taking steps to correct the issues that are identified. Issues resolved using this process are referred to as analytical problems and require solutions that comply with certain identified standards. Toyota, too, is trying to solve these types of problems just like many other companies using a Kaizen change management process. For example, Ford takes 3 hours to complete a production process changeover, while another company doing a similar process requires 3.5 hours. This realization leads them to identify and analyze the problem. Next, using some type of improvement process they were able to shorten the work time on their own process to 2 hours 55 minutes. They felt that the problem was resolved, and the issue they were focused on became invisible. With that the improvement story came to an end.

However, in the case of Toyota, applying its thinking habit of ultimate thinking, it flips the invisible problem and makes it visible realizing that comprehending the problem and working on it further became the challenge. This significantly differs from the thinking habit of others. Instead, Toyota focuses on single-digit minute changeover. It does not focus on comparative benchmarking, where the goal is being slightly better than the competition. Instead, Toyota looks toward the ultimate goal. It sees the goal of its improvement effort as one improvement, which is to shorten the original changeover times of 3.5 hours to just 3 minutes. The ultimate and ideal state is zero time and this would be the second level of an improvement effort. This ultimate state is the improved performance goal that still needs to be achieved. The problem, from a Toyota perspective, is not how bad it is. Rather, the focus is on the difference between the ideal state and the current state. This type of problem is referred to as an opportunity developing problem and the use of ultimate thinking brings more opportunity development problems to the surface requiring attention. For Toyota, the occurrence of a problem is not regarded as something embarrassing. Rather, it is considered a challenge offering the opportunity for additional progress.

USING ULTIMATE THINKING TO ACHIEVE NEVER-ENDING KAIZEN

My Life and Work by Henry Ford, the founder of Ford Motor Company, was said to be one of Kiichiro Toyoda's favorite books. In his book Henry Ford wrote the following:

> If to petrify is success all one has to do is to humour the lazy side of the mind but if to grow is success, then one must wake up anew every morning and keep awake all day. I saw great businesses become but the ghost of a name because someone thought they could be managed just as they were always managed, and though the management may have been most excellent in its day, its excellence consisted in its alertness to its day, and not in slavish following of its yesterdays. Life, as I see it, is not a location, but a journey. Even the man who most feels himself "settled" is not settled—he is probably sagging back. Everything is in flux, and was meant to be. Life flows. We may live at the same number of the street, but it is never the same man who lives there.

Few people, including Toyoda, dare to deny Ford's words. It is apparent that Toyoda was inspired by Ford's book. It encouraged him to creatively search for ways to build an ever-changing (continuously improving) Toyota. This process resulted in the Toyota ultimate thinking approach, as shown in its creation of the just-in-time practice.

The use of the ultimate thinking paradigm can ensure continuous change. Looking back at Figure 8.1 we see that there is a large gap between the current and the ultimate (ideal) states. Filling this gap calls for a series of improvement activities as well as a lot of creative thinking. Catching up with other companies generally will not allow us to reach the ultimate state. More improvement plans and change implementations are needed. Achieving the goal of zero is an endless challenge, and it requires a seamless stream of improvements before the zero target is achieved.

When zero is finally achieved, another target will get your attention. It is exactly like mountain climbing. When you get to the top of one mountain, you find the next mountain that you want to climb (a new goal), always stretching yourself to attain the summit. By using ultimate thinking we identify larger and larger gaps. Thus, ultimate thinking creates chances to explore new opportunities, one after another, regardless of what other companies do. Ultimately your organization will discover that it has achieved the position of top runner. Ultimate thinking leads to a transformation, changing the organization into a learning organization with relentless reflections and tireless improvements.

The authors of this book have offered guidance to many organizations and corporations with a focus on driving them to create "super top runner strategies" utilizing the tools of continuous innovation discussed in this book. The core concept has been to introduce the thinking habits of "thinking and identifying the essence of the process or the system," and then applying ultimate thinking. Toyota's thinking habits have completely incorporated this ultimate thinking approach and made it a habit.

STRUGGLING FOR IDEAS IS NECESSARY TO GAIN WISDOM

Another pillar of Toyota's thinking habits that are outlined in "The Toyota Way 2001" is to think creatively using ingenuity. Knowledge can be increased by applying wisdom and studying, but wisdom cannot be built only by book learning. Taiichi Ohno often said to his subordinates, "You can always find solutions. But your ingenuity is the most creative when you are in trouble." He had asked them to acquire his thinking habit that believes that ingenuity appears only when being pinched. Toyota's thinking habit believes its wisdom starts working best when workers are put into the position of having no other choice. That's when ingenuity kicks in.

Toyota uses the ultimate thinking habit when it encounters problem situations. Kiichiro Toyoda should have received resistance from his people when he presented them with the ultimate (ideal) states of no inventory and just-in-time production management. He expected them to make excuses, grumbling and saying, "Boss, that's impossible. Even Ford runs their business with three months of inventory." For those who lack a willingness to be inventive, there is little chance for success and ingenuity. Ohno had always focused on identifying solutions for his boss's challenging questions. He focused on thinking, thinking, and more thinking. He drove toward ingenuity. One day he read an industrial journal article on supermarket operations, a new concept in America. Supermarkets inspired him and, looking closely at their operations, he came up with his concept of a kanban system. This system interacted with the preceding processes in order to get resupplied in parts. The book's author Noguchi remembers taking Ohno to one of the supermarkets in Los Angeles and taking a close look at their operations.

Ultimate thinking may seem ridiculous, almost to the point of harassment to some people, because it demands that they achieve something that seems impossible. But a thinking habit of no compromise is one of the qualities inherited from the thinking habits of the traditional Mikawa warriors.

People at Toyota are said to suffer from an affliction referred to as being solution-aholics. This addiction drives them to think and drive toward ingenuity. They are blamed for this affliction because they are continuously in a state of searching for and identifying problems (opportunities for improvement), one after another. They strive to find opportunities that will allow them to use ultimate thinking. In other words, Toyota's employees are placed in an environment where they have no other choice but to work hard using their ingenuity night and day. This behavior leads to their receiving the label of being solution-aholics.

TOYOTA'S FUTURE PULL

In and around us, at home or at work, there are many types of inventory in many different forms. Taking the perspective of a model with shelves, where we would have a shelf representing the past, a shelf for the present, and a shelf for the future, which shelf is fullest for us? In the case of a nearly bankrupt business enterprise, the shelf of the past must be full of dead inventory. A company struggling with an excessive amount of current jobs must have its present shelf the fullest. And a company focused on the future of the company and searching for growth opportunities would be the fullest on the future shelf. Unfortunately, far too many companies today have their future shelf nearly empty. Since they lack future inventory, they are unable to accurately project their course moving forward. They are losing their momentum and heading for bankruptcy. They are meandering around without clear direction. We need to understand how critical the inventory that is on the future shelf really is before going to the next topic.

The "shelf of the future" concept was derived from the triangle of ideal future solutions discussed earlier. The base of this triangle refers to the shelf where we keep present day concepts, processes, and activities. The concepts at this bottom level are all immediately executable without any effort to modify or improve them. The next level up is called the level of target concepts, which are tools that are technologically feasible today. We need to identify a target concept or system for each of them. Even higher than these on the next level up are concepts calling for technological development and they are referred to as technology-fiction concepts. An example of this would be the phone chip, which will be introduced someday after the development of some critically technical elements like supersmall power cells. This shelf level is where we would place and search for target concepts. Above that, at the upper level, we find the world of fantastic fiction or dreams. It is the shelf of the ultimate and ideal future solutions.

The shelf of the future should contain a time axis from the bottom to the top indicating the different levels of feasibility. It is also appropriate to organize the future shelves by type. We are familiar with a company that developed a system that organized everything related to a specific concept, like its description, pictures, and drawings. All of this was available by the click of a button on its PC. It included detailed data and information all stored on its computer system. It is getting easier to organize search capabilities that will link these functions to the web.

The future shelf can contain simple ideas, but over time these ideas should be developed into sophisticated concepts with specific identities, starting with a name. These concepts should be organized in such a way that target concepts can be aligned with future strategies. It would also be useful to list these concepts by type, or to organize them and link them together as variations or models of similar concepts and create a concept series. This does not need to be in the form of a triangle. It can also be graphically represented as a rectangle so that it looks more like a real shelf. It is our recommendation that readers have their own future shelves with room for various designs and concepts. It is valuable to understand the importance of using the tool referred to here as a future shelf. A future shelf is simply a navigation chart that assists in clarifying the course we are to take.

You will discover something interesting when you make your own shelf of the future. Those who only talk about the future will find that their concepts are only visible on the uppermost shelf. Other individuals who are preoccupied with the present will have all their concepts stored on the bottom shelf with very little on the top. These extremes indicate the need to think about and project more ideas that will fill out concepts and ideas across all the shelves, from the top, through the middle, and down to the bottom.

There is another critical point to be made about these shelves of the future. The concepts lodged on each different shelf exist to fulfill and satisfy a purpose and to create value. They are yardsticks that we use to measure the accomplishment of our purposes. They are target values. That implies that they are guaranteed to be successful when they are eventually implemented. The shelf is not just about dreams. There needs to be a significant direction for our concepts and ideas when we are designing our future. There should be a popular cry of "Let's brainstorm about our future. Let's dream about what we could be."

FUTURE SOLUTIONS AND IDEAL SOLUTIONS IN THE AUTOMOBILE MARKET

Toyota refers to this future shelf as its future drawers. Akio Toyoda, the current president of Toyota Motors, expressed his determination to identify and respond to a wider variety of choices for consumers in different regions. That was in his future drawer. Masanao Shiomi, former executive of Toyota for engineering, expressed these thoughts at a forum presentation: "We can identify and create fuel cells that will function for long-distance travel. Compact and short-distance drives should be left to electric vehicles where we use hybrid and plug-in hybrid designs for passenger cars. ... We need to offer different types of vehicles from which our customers can choose."

A narrative description of ideal future solutions applied to the automotive industry would be as follows:

> Mr. Yamada along with his family is driving en route to the popular restaurant Kanayama in Ginza, Tokyo, for a dinner party. They are driving down the Second Tomei Expressway. The vehicle they are driving is a new Toyota Alfa autonomous drive model using fuel cells. They are ready to leave but they first stop by a hydrogen station for refueling which takes about two minutes. The car drives itself using an artificial intelligence guidance system and there is no steering wheel in the vehicle. All he has to do is tell the car where he wants to go using voice command. It starts the car and begins to drive itself, entering the highway toward its destination. Inside the car,

the passengers enjoy high-fidelity music as if they were in a concert hall. Or they can be watching movies or reading books. The car is connected with the web. The passengers enjoy being in their car and soon discover that they have arrived in Ginza, Tokyo. After the dinner party, they can nap inside their car during their return drive home. At the end of the trip the car parks itself back into its garage.

This story is feasible enough in the near future. It comes from the future drawers of Toyota. However, this story only becomes possible by applying the absolute benchmarks of no environmental destruction and no accidents.

PARTS ACQUISITION AS A PART OF GLOBAL MARKETING

Global application of the types of future solutions described in this chapter were initiated within Toyota with the start of the New United Motor Manufacturing Inc. (NUMMI) project, a joint venture with General Motors in the United States.

NUMMI started with initial local content of 50%, including Toyota-supplied engines and transmissions. Its goal after 5 years was to raise local content to include the engine, transmission, air conditioners, and other key components so that it would raise the local content to over 75%. The ultimate guidelines given by Kiichiro Toyoda, as mentioned earlier, were disclosed to the American parts suppliers as ideal future solutions. The fundamentals of the NUMMI purchasing policy are as follows:

1. Customer satisfaction is No. 1—Toyoda aimed at the ultimate state of management by objectively using a market survey focused on identifying customer needs and which incorporated a merchandising plan based on the PDCA cycle. He validated the customer's level of satisfaction utilizing other additional surveys.
2. Air pollution control—He focused on the ultimate ideal state, which eliminates all pollutant emissions.
3. Scarcity of resource and fuel economy—He developed improved gasoline-free car engines such as hydrogen fuel cell cars and electric cars.

4. Safety and accident free—In addition to more stringent traffic regulations and improved roads, he put more emphasis on connected cars and autonomous driving device development (artificial intelligence-assisted vehicle control).

5. More family orientation—He focused on trying to become better neighbors. He organized a series of social events, such as picnics, dinner parties, and sporting events, which promoted a team spirit.

Initially U.S. parts suppliers kept their production processes a secret. The majority of Western suppliers, including Michelin and TRW, were not allowing outsiders to see their plants. Nondisclosure of their privately developed and privately branded production processes was a common practice of those corporations, and they appealed to the U.S. Department of Commerce as Toyota required the disclosure of their processes as a condition for procurement. Initially most of them had no interest in improving their processes. They already felt that they had identified their own exclusive expertise.

Toyota, based on its firm belief that quality should be built into the process, persisted in requiring that they disclose their processes. In the years that followed, those suppliers relented and started to disclose their processes, especially after Toyota identified a poor performance record for their quality and cost. They came to understand why Toyota wanted to understand their processes and started to work together for the betterment of both parties. They worked with Toyota's experts. Their relationship was transformed into a win–win relationship, as demonstrated by the following examples of results that were achieved:

1. Reduction in in-process inventories
2. Reduction in cost
3. Improved quality
4. Changes in the work mode with more collaboration and more opportunities for improvements
5. Enhanced visibility of the future of the industry

In the following years, such Japanese parts suppliers like Denso, Sango, Aisin, Koito, Maruyasu, and many more went to the United States to establish their expatriate corporations. Soon they also became American suppliers. In the meantime, we have seen an increasing number of joint ventures between Japanese and American suppliers like ARVIN-Sango and others.

Toyota has motivated suppliers with an incentive scheme centered on management by objectives to reflect their performance. Readers of this book must come to understand the sixth ingredient behind the strength of Toyota. It is its "ultimate thinking" practice.

TOYOTA'S GLOBAL MARKETING STRATEGY: SECRET INGREDIENT #6

A principle of the Breakthrough Thinking—Pursue an ideal state starting with a fundamental foundation. Learn from the ideal states and project them into the future. Start to think in terms of ultimate and ideal states. Focus on absolute benchmarks.

At this point it is also useful to review the seven principles of Breakthrough Thinking, which are

1. Uniqueness
2. Purposeful information
3. Systems
4. People involvement
5. Purpose
6. Future solution
7. Living solution

Details about these seven principles and their application are discussed in the following books:

Breakthrough Thinking: The Seven Principles of Creative Problem Solving, by Gerald Nadler and Shozo Hibino, 1994

Making Innovation Happen: Concept Management through Integration, by Gerhard J. Plenert and Shozo Hibino, 1997

Conventional wisdom—Learn from the past and the present. Learn from the best practices of others in your specific business sector. You can find a stack of business books teaching successful case examples in every bookstore. Most people are desperately trying to emulate the success stories of others. They also use relative benchmarking to set up targets allowing them to compare themselves with other companies.

At Toyota—As this book has pointed out several times, Toyota has effectively been using the principle of ultimate thinking in the development of the Toyota Production System. Whatever you call it, whether it's Toyota's ultimate thinking, ideal thinking, the theory of ideal states, the vision of the desired state, or something else, Toyota has been employing its hybrid thinking habit, which keeps it focused on seamless improvements and innovation. It is continuously in pursuit of the ideal future solution with an eye focused on the essence of what is being produced.

Question for Reflection

Discuss why marketing strategies should incorporate absolute benchmarking or ideal future solutions.

9

Secret Ingredient #7: When Progressing toward Ideal Future Solutions, Confront the Present— The Living Solution Principle

A solution developed using the process of reductionist thinking is just like creating a blueprint that never changes. On the other hand, one of the perspectives and tools of Breakthrough Thinking is that there is no such thing as a perfect and everlasting applicable solution. There is never only one answer to a problem. Rather, it defines a solution to be more like a motion picture that is constantly changing. As our world is constantly in motion, a solution cannot be eternally unchangeable. The application of any solution should be adapted constantly while continuing to improve daily, weekly, monthly, and annually. Achieving a state of mind where we recognize this continuous change leads us to recognize the impermanence of all things, which is an ancient Buddhism philosophy.

After all, the ultimate goal of applying Breakthrough Thinking is the creation of living solutions, which means flexibility in our response to our ever-changing conditions. We must remember to implement our solutions with a focus and direction aimed at the ideal future solutions. Accordingly, we need to create living solutions that are executable in the real world while learning from the ideal future solutions. More specifically, we need to identify time schedules that motivate us to achieve our current solutions within the agreed upon time spans, such as 1 year, 2 years, 5 years, 10 years, you name it. Ultimately the goal is to reach the ideal future solution in this timeline. This is the opposite concept when considering conventional reductionism where we focus our thinking on a future that is a fixed and immovable state, much like a blueprint.

MOVING TOWARD IDEAL FUTURE SOLUTIONS USING NEVER-ENDING KAIZEN

This book's author Shozo Hibino was once asked the following question from a developing country trainee that he was teaching. The trainee said, "My country's intellectual class enjoys deep discussions. They meet every evening over alcohol talking lively about various issues. I have no objection to this tradition because it is positive for the growth of our country. But they never do anything with the solutions that they come up with. The solutions never get turned into practice. They continue their discussions on the next day, often on the same topic, but the results are shelved. All these ideas are being sidelined without anything getting implemented. They never change anything. There is no implemented solution and no improvement. What do you suggest we should do professor?"

What do you the reader think about this individual's concerns? This situation is not unique to this particular developing country. We see many cases of this in many locations. Many people discuss options and solutions and do nothing. The conversations go from one topic to the next, each time coming up with excellent ideas, but they never put any of these ideas into practice. The result is that there are no implemented plans to improve the country. Unfortunately, we even see this same trend in advanced countries.

Toyota's thinking habit calls for a revolving cycle of "ingenuity, practice, awareness, and improvement" and it rejects the deskbound discussions that never get executed. They require immediate practical application. They look for the implementation of creative ideas where individual ingenuity has been applied. This increases awareness, which leads to and encourages the next improvement, followed by even more creativeness put into practice, increased awareness, and continuous improvement. Ideally this cycle goes on and on without end. The critical factors in making this cycle work are as follows:

1. Be creative—Do not imitate or use comparative benchmarking. Do not shop catalogs for ideas. Be creative by applying ingenuity and focus on the ideal future solutions.
2. Put it into practice—No result or improvement is validated without giving it a try. You should have the spirit of experimentation. You can always return to the previous state if your improvement attempt does not work.

3. Awareness—If you are aware of the essence of the situation, you can focus the direction of your improvement and you can make your fundamental improvement feasible. Awareness does not mean imitation. You should always be working with your own original ideas.

This cycle of creativity, followed by putting your idea into practice, and always being aware of the situation so you can properly validate the improvement, should become a repeated cycle so that you maintain a system of seamless and continuous improvement, eventually leading you toward your ideal future solution.

THINKING HABITS THAT MOTIVATE PEOPLE

The engine for driving Toyota's continuous improvement system is a two-fold mechanism of (1) managing by making it visible (visualization), and (2) ultimate thinking (as previously discussed).

Both the kanban system and the 5S campaign are mechanisms dedicated to making problems and waste visible. When your work location is organized and clean, and after removing everything that is not needed in order to accomplish you job, the in-process activates and materials become visible and tangible. When your problems and wastes become visible, you can identify opportunities for improvement and start working toward solutions. You start applying your creativity and ingenuity, begin planning solutions, start practicing them, and get awareness of the results related to the changes to see if you really made an improvement. As more problems and wastes become recognized, you will have no choice but to keeping practicing a seamless continuous improvement process.

Another mechanism is found in their ultimate thinking. Being ultimate means either achieving 0 or 100%. As previously mentioned, when setup and changeover times can be reduced from 3 hours to just 3 minutes, it still should not be sufficient to completely satisfy us. The 3 minutes should be reduced even more to 2 minutes; the 2 minutes should be shortened to 1 minute; 1 minute down to 30 seconds, and so on. It requires constant and repeated improvement reductions. The current practices of other companies like Ford and GM did not justify Toyota's need for improvement. Toyota focused its thinking habits on continuous improvement and this became its inherent appetite. Its ultimate and ideal state is to eliminate all setup and changeover work and drive it down to zero. When it succeed in arriving at a zero processing time, Toyota entered the next stage of its continuous improvement process where it identified other areas that are not yet at zero and started another series of continuous improvements on that activity. When you acquire Toyota's thinking habit, you will not be able to escape from becoming a solution-aholic too.

Toyota values humanity. It does not employ people and treat them like robotic mechanisms, but it treats people as living beings with intelligence. It creates situations in which its people feel thrilled by being able to strive to constantly and repeatedly identifying new improvements. The reason of those crazy hard-working Toyota people is not because they are being forced by a management by an objectives approach, but simply because they feel joy in the work that they do. Seamless improvement is not a duty. Rather it helps them to discover the excitement and pleasure of inventing and creating. It motivates them.

TOYOTA'S ENEMY IS ITSELF

In the world of sports, any star athlete's primary competitor is always oneself. When you are at the top and at the highest level of competition, the struggle is within yourself. For example, in a marathon you push yourself, or in boxing you train yourself, and so on. Kosuke Shiramizu, former executive vice president of Toyota Motor, wrote in his article in the *JMA Management Review*: "At the onset of 2001, Hiroshi Okuda, chairman of our company, gave a new guiding message to each and every management officer. The message was to 'defeat Toyota,' by which he meant, 'the Toyota of tomorrow should reject and transform the Toyota of the past. Otherwise our company cannot win against its global competition.'" Hiroshi Okuda expressed his sense of crisis and urgency. He focused on the need for being unable to respond to a future rapidly changing environment in both the areas of quality and response time.

Shiramizu continued, "It is true that our superior mindset is inclined to search for improvements and that this mindset has been diffused to everyone from rank and file operators through to management within the company. We have been admired in and out of this country for our performance in producing and in continuous improvement." However, his latest message was an eye-opening directive, especially for those who had simply believed that the victory had already been won. This new message stressed that to continue winning the global race would require an ongoing effort. Toyota cannot rest on its past successes. It must continue to creatively strive toward the future. The future cannot simply be an extension of the present.

The awareness shown in Kosuke Shiramizu's message called for a transformation of the conventional recognition of Toyota. Kosuke Shiramizu clearly stated that the primary competitor of Toyota was Toyota itself, rather than GM, Ford, Nissan, or Honda. From that moment on, Toyota boldly changed direction and started its intensive practice toward becoming a breakthrough Toyota organization. It focused on a new thinking engine and a new thinking habit. Just as when it created the Toyota Production System, it now needed to break new ground in the creation of the next generation Toyota Corporation.

SQUEEZE OR CHANGE?

The practice of wringing the water out of a dry rag has always been an inherent part of Toyota's thinking habits. This concept, in a few words, expresses Toyota's uncompromising focus on cost reduction. Cost reduction reaches an extreme state where you find yourself unable to cut any more costs. Toyota labels this state as a dry rag and persists in asking for further wringing even though it is dry just in case there is one more drop. This demonstrates the need for an even more thorough focus on cost reduction. When this book's author Hibino visited Toyota in the 1970s, he asked the top management of Toyota, "What would you do when your rag has been wrung so much that one more wringing will rip it?" The Toyota executive replied, "That might happen. However if you keep it for a while, it will absorb more moisture from the air and you can wring it again." The reply statement is a manifestation of Toyota's thinking habit demonstrating a belief that it is always necessary to wring out the rag, even if you think it is a dry rag. Moisture will eventually creep in.

Toyota has evolved to the point where it recognizes that wringing a dry rag is simply not sufficient. Sometimes it is necessary to change the rag. This demonstrates a process of continuously improving, even if the improvement is in the thinking habits. Toyota realizes that it must not just improve as an extension of its past practices, but it will not stay on top of world markets unless its makes cars that incorporate entirely new concepts, such as hybrid cars and fuel cell cars. This is necessary while at the same time creating new business models and adopting new ways of production that include even going beyond the successful Toyota Production System.

It would be easier to understand Toyota's transformation if we further understand its thinking habit of wringing out a dry rag. This concept represents a conventional approach to management by continuous improvement. Exchanging the rag after its extreme use suggests an innovative management approach leading to a breakthrough and breakaway Toyota. For management by continuous improvement, conventional reductionist thinking (induction) is an effective tool. However, innovative management calls for using Breakthrough Thinking (deduction) as the approach for driving fundamental organizational change. It is correct that we still need to wring out the dry rag, but we should also recognize that at some point it becomes critical to exchange the rag. In a nutshell, today's Toyota needs a hybrid thinking engine. Historically, figures like Ieyasu Tokugawa, Nobunaga Oda, Sakichi Toyoda, and Kiichiro Toyoda already had the improvement and innovation thinking habit. But this needed to be strengthened throughout the remainder of the Toyota employees.

Many critics do not understand Toyota's thinking habits. They criticize its innovation campaign because they confuse it with the previous thinking habit of wringing a rag, which was an extension of past practices. These people are missing the essential point of how the innovation campaign works. There are even individuals within Toyota, including top-ranking officials, that misunderstand its meaning because of how ingrained the wringing rag doctrine was for them. The authors of this book would like them to go back to Toyota's original thinking habits that were inherited from Sakichi and Kiichiro Toyoda over many generations and rethink what they actually believed.

An old proverb says "The wise individual changes his mind three times a day. An idiot never changes. ... The wise can adapt themselves to a changing environment." Changing ideas three times in a day allows us to discover and learn something new, and to create new solutions three times in the same day. An idiot, on the other hand, is unable to create and change anything. In our current turbulence, those who are concerned with Toyota wish to incorporate and ingrain the thinking habit of daily innovation along with daily improvement. Readers of this book are advised to find the benefits of identifying and incorporating a hybrid thinking engine, which consists of two different thinking modes.

Sadly, people find it challenging to follow the concepts of daily improvement and daily innovation. The authors of this book are facilitating the integration of these concepts into many companies. Daily improvement and daily innovation uses Breakthrough Thinking as its foundational implementation method. We often see people saying, "Why should we push ahead with these new ideas? Why are we changing something that already works well?" People resist change both physically and psychologically. Even within Toyota it is easy to find some individuals who resist waves of improvement and innovation. However, within Toyota in general, most employees have successfully accepted the thinking habits of daily improvement and innovation, which follow the traditional philosophies that come down from the days of Sakichi and Kiichiro Toyoda. These have successfully taken root inside the company because of its culture of continuous change.

ASK WHETHER YOU HAVE TAKEN THE NEXT STEP

This is a time when numerous companies who were at one time labeled as excellent companies are finding themselves struggling and often filing bankruptcy. Sears, Roebuck, & Co. had annual sales of US$3.6 billion and was the leader in the retail industry for over a hundred years. It was a beloved and undoubtedly extremely successful American business corporation. Unfortunately the company had to dismiss its over 50,000 employees when its stock price collapsed and it was forced to file for bankruptcy. Similarly in Japan there have been corporations that have found themselves in crisis and have been forced into bankruptcy. In the past two decades these corporations, including companies like Sharp Corporation, that were believed to be immune from collapse, found themselves in trouble.

Is there a solution? Actually it might be inappropriate to use the term *solution*. Instead, it would be more meaningful and it would give us a clearer picture of the situation if we asked questions like, what does this problem (or this challenge or this failure) mean? A problem is "a state that calls for change." Accordingly, it is appropriate to rephrase the initial question of "Is there a solution?" to something like "Is there an appropriate change?" or better yet "Is there an appropriate change that is required?" If we use the term *change*, then we imply that there is a something to be changed and that the change moves us toward a solution. It is increasingly critical to recognize that a solution requires a change and that this is a critical realization during our current turbulent times and on into the new century.

Figure 9.1 graphically shows us how growth should progress. Using Breakthrough Thinking, we can select target 1 as some future ideal state. Then, we put it into practice to achieve improved success. However, soon other competitors find it as well and start to catch up with you. The competition makes it necessary to discover why we need to incorporate the principle of ever-changing solutions (The Living Solution Principle). Unless you take the next initiative moving yourself forward continuously ahead of the competition, you will find yourself exhausted by being in direct competition with your rivals. In the end, competing neck to neck will run you into bankruptcy. Too many business ventures go bankrupt because they are unable to apply the principle of continuous innovation even if they were initially able to succeed with their ideas. Breakthrough Thinking calls for continuously preparing for the next ideal state after the next ideal state, even if you think you are currently in an ideal state. It is important to take effective next-step measures after the first stage, then again after the second stage, and the third stage, and so on in order to ensure continuous expansion (Figures 9.2 and 9.3).

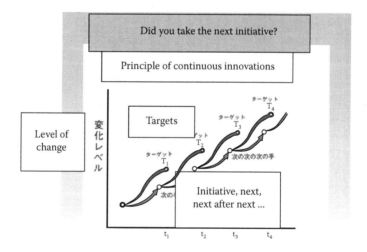

FIGURE 9.1
Principle of continuously changing living solutions.

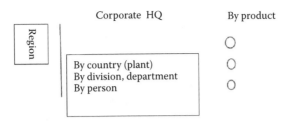

FIGURE 9.2
The Toyota competitive approach.

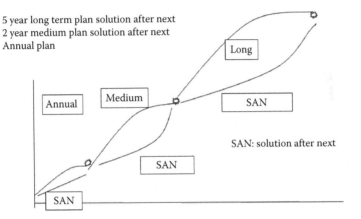

FIGURE 9.3
Solution after next planning.

The late Steve Jobs of Apple grew an innovative company by launching new products one after another, like the Mac, iPod, iPhone, iPad, and the rest. However, more recently Apple has been sluggish. Is it because the company has not continued in taking on next-stage initiatives after the demise of Jobs? We are all entering into a new age when we need twofold strategies that will get us both "food for today and food for tomorrow." To become a super top runner, we should keep continuous innovation firmly in our mind. It requires the thinking habit where we ask ourselves, "Did I take the next step initiative?" as well as asking, "Do I have the next after the next step initiative?"

ORGANIZING GLOBAL MARKETING

In order to apply Toyota's thinking habits outside of Japan, the book's author Koichiro Noguchi tried to implement living solutions with a goal of identifying and moving toward the ultimate ideal state just the way Kiichiro Toyoda first advocated. Noguchi identified the following three types of ultimate target values and used them as guidelines for the supervision of his staff:

1. Customer satisfaction—100%
2. Air pollution—Zero (only water is discharged when using hydrogen energy)
3. Fossil fuels—Zero (using hydrogen and oxygen energy)

Growth of a business organization lies in the development of its people. Keeping Breakthrough Thinking and breakthrough tools as our watchword, Noguchi asked each department to compile mission statements and made them perform and be measured against these statements in order to measure their achievement. Consequently they were assessed based on a target-achievement performance and treated as one Toyota group. When hydrogen energy was identified as the way to satisfy these goals and became Toyota's new target area for innovation, it was quickly released and published in all the newspapers.

Future innovations will be focused on information and communications technology (ICT) applications, where vehicles incorporate autonomous driving solutions. IBM, a top manufacturer of the 1990s, used Intel as a parts supplier and Intel advertised it on their computers saying "Intel Inside." Soon Intel, having the core technologies of the computer, became a top runner in the computer industry in the 2000s and IBM became just the manufacturer of steel cases. Hibino guided Hitachi Automotive using Breakthrough Thinking and it soon developed a "Hitachi Inside" brand by incorporating core technologies for autonomous drive vehicles. Hitachi tried to sell these devices as a whole system to medium-ranked car assemblers who had limited resources. Even Toyota needs to face the challenge of new technology development with its own initiative if they are to prevent their automobile sector from becoming just the assembler of steel boxes. Toyota would need to develop new technological applications that are ahead of their time to become the critical pieces for cars of the future, which are calling for more innovations including artificial intelligence and networking. Noguchi wishes to see Toyota's further growth while observing and recognizing its next wave of challenges.

TOYOTA'S NEXT STEPS

Toyota has used its empirical and continuous improvement projects in its push to become No. 1 in the world. Its overall productivity has increased in parallel with its historical milestones, such as entry into overseas markets, which includes the development of new models, and a full-fledge expansion into the markets of many developing nations. It started overseas production by launching new plants in numerous international locations and worked closely in collaboration with other automobile makers both inside and outside of Japan. It nurtured the growth and development of its overseas employee base of human resources and shared Toyota's technical information. It did all of these things and many more while growing its market share and expanding the size of its employee base. Now Toyota is at the point of seeking for ways to create new values that are not encumbered with the past. It is searching for a new perspective. The authors of this book hope to see Toyota facing new challenges that incorporate innovative and creative plans aimed at ideal future solutions, as elaborated in the previous chapter.

The next-step tasks for Toyota toward its future are artificial intelligence, IOT (Internet of Things) of manufacturing, computerization of cars, hacking control legislation, and cars free from exhaust pollutions.

Artificial Intelligence: Autonomous Drive Technologies

The first technology needed as Toyota pursues its ideal future solutions is artificial intelligence. This would be the core for data and information processing. The book's author Hibino was creating innovations for Toyota at Chukyo University using Breakthrough Thinking in the mid-1980s when NUMMI (New United Motor Manufacturing Inc.) was inaugurated. At that time he was already focusing on artificial intelligence. The technology was still in its early stages. At that time Hibino attempted to establish a new School of Artificial Intelligence (AI) and made an application to the Japanese government, but the Ministry of Education responded with a request for him to change its name, as the desired name was considered to be beyond the ability of the ministry to accept it as feasible. Hibino, accordingly, decided to launch his own new lab of artificial intelligence in Chukyo University that focused on AI research by inviting participation from the private sector, specifically for autonomous drive vehicles. Since then collaboration between academic and business institutions has become common practice. Traditionally it was thought to be impossible to invite businesses to a university campus because of the economic dependency it would create. In spite of that tradition, Hibino approached several companies including Toyota and initiated a collaborative effort. Toyota introduced these plans to Denso and an AI research program was started at Chukyo University in conjunction with the start of a research and development (R&D) center for AI within Toyota. From these early beginnings, Toyota has now commenced a full-scale R&D effort focused on AI.

Toyota set up the Toyota Research Institute, Inc. (TRI) in San Jose, California, in the area known as Silicon Valley. TRI is undertaking AI studies with four goals:

1. Accident-free cars
2. Cars for all ages
3. Indoor robots where mobility technology is applied
4. Accelerated study of science and principles by utilizing artificial intelligence and machine learning

Toyota has also reexamined its previous approach focused on doing everything in-house and launched collaborative research projects in about 30 subject areas with Stanford University and Massachusetts Institute of Technology (MIT). Toyota has clearly changed its stance in its pursuit of ideal future solutions with these relationships.

The development of autonomous driving technology is evolving in stages. Level 1 refers to autonomous acceleration, steering, and control including collision prevention. Several corporations have begun researching and introducing these applications into their own vehicles. The next level calls for autonomously controlled high-speed cruise capabilities for highways, and Toyota plans to have this capability available by the year 2020. The third level is the development of autonomous driving vehicles for normal street driving. This level raises more technical challenges including the revision of the legal systems in order to manage accident liabilities. Then, the next stage in driving technology would be the development of fully autonomous driving cars without any driver seats. This is the ideal future solution that was envisioned in the previous chapter. This would be the ultimate autonomous car and can only be built after solving numerous challenges such as the development of stereoscopic mapping.

IOT (Internet of Things) of Manufacturing

Toyota has taken the manufacturing lead over its competitors by its more advanced manufacturing processes that have achieved world-class performance, such as demonstrated by the kanban system or its cellular manufacturing system. However, as in the case of artificial intelligence, even though the Toyota Production System triggered process innovation in the past, it is also continuously changing into the future. The original concept focused on getting parts resupplied in exchange for a sheet of paper called a kanban. This is going to be replaced by the e-kanban. The advent of the Internet has brought with it enormous changes in the production processes. One example of these emerging changes is the Internet of Things (IOT). The IOT is a structured system of various stages and interactions within the production process. These interactions are connected by the Internet and the exchange of information is used to ensure mutual control of the overall process. "Industry 4.0," advocated by the German government, has the potential to trigger even more innovation in the area of production systems processes. Toyota needs to reexamine its processes and take appropriate action by asking itself, Can we win in the next stage of production transformations using the current methodology and systems that are part of Japanese manufacturing? Rather than limiting itself within its Toyota Production System, which is supposed to keep evolving by adopting artificial intelligence and the IOT, there is an even larger leap beyond what currently exists. For instance, the current Toyota Production System halts an assembly line using the andon mechanism. However, today it is feasible to detect a potential failure in advance of the actual failure by employing AI and the IOT, thereby keeping the assembly line operating 24 hours a day and 365 days a year allowing for an even more ideal state for production using just-in-time.

The authors of this book believe that reinventing its production processes will be a critical task for Toyota in the coming year, allowing it to continue in the development of new ways of manufacturing and marketing, thereby maintaining its excellent level of corporate performances. This would also maintain the momentum initiated by their predecessors who inherited the thinking habits that we previously connected with the founders of Toyota.

Computerization of Cars

Another critical technology toward Toyota's ideal future vehicle solutions is the computerized car. Toyota, in collaboration with Microsoft, is working hard to develop the concept of connected cars. Most carmakers have adopted Google's Android Auto technology, whereas only Toyota has joined hands with Microsoft, creating a concern about the connectivity of Toyota cars with the rest of the world's cars. Hibino knows that NEC has been focusing on its own software technologies but eventually even this Japanese company had to switch to Microsoft Windows when it worked as consultants for other companies. Using this example, Toyota might find it necessary to create its own solutions to ensure its connectivity with the other automakers before it is too late. Microsoft is good at PCs, but it is running behind Google's Android Auto in the area of net connectivity including technologies like smartphones. Toyota needs to become involved with other car assemblers as it moves forward in its development of technologies like Microsoft Auto or Toyota Net Auto if it is to be adopted as the new international standard.

Toyota will need to develop more advanced car information systems terminals to handle topographical mapping, high-fidelity music playback, and e-book browsing in its vehicles, as was introduced previously in this book where we discussed versatile functionality within artificial intelligence.

Hacking Control Legislation

The more advanced the computerization of cars becomes with tools like artificial intelligence, the higher the potential risks and hazards of hacking. If autonomous driving is hacked, it may affect the safety of humans and destroy the brand image of Toyota. Because of this, hacking control becomes critical. We currently do not have laws that govern cases surrounding accidents involving autonomous driving vehicles and what should happen in the case where they are targeted by hacking. This requires legislature and we should ask the legislative branch of our governments to consider these new requirements and to enact new laws to adapt to the changes of the times.

Cars Free from Exhaust Pollutions

Toyota has announced its long-term plans to stop almost all sales of cars running only with gasoline by 2050. According to these plans, Toyota will introduce different types of vehicles in the following sequence:

1. High-mileage gasoline fuel vehicles
2. Hybrid vehicles
3. Plug-in hybrid vehicles
4. Fuel cell vehicles

Toyota focused on achieving a state of zero emissions to the environment by 2050, but then it discovered that the American automotive industry had already started to become serious about electric vehicles. This resulted from legislation focused on zero-emission vehicles (ZEVs). This legislation quickly spread over nine states including California and New York. Initially, plug-in hybrid models were included in the ZEV category. Then it was learned that hybrid cars would not be approved as ZEV starting in 2018, and Toyota was suddenly forced to accelerate its development of electric vehicles. Originally, hybrid vehicles, plug-in hybrids, and fuel cell vehicles had common technological elements with electric vehicles. This meant that it should not be too difficult for Toyota to develop a full-scale electric vehicle. Technologies for hybrid cars required the ability for the vehicle to run on both gasoline engines and electric motors. That makes the development more complicated, and companies that are new to the marketplace would discover that this is a big burden to overcome. In comparison, the electric vehicle's structure is much simpler, and companies late to enter the market would find it easier to become viable. However, we still needed the innovation of improved, long-lasting batteries that only time will solve. Fuel cell vehicles will require the development of a new infrastructure, like the development of hydrogen "fuel stations." This will be more challenging for countries like the United States who are behind in the creation of this technology, and they need to put more emphasis on shifting their attention to electric vehicles. Tesla, specializing in electric vehicles, has already marketed its compact sedan Model S that can run as long as 350 km per power charge, and it was swamped with a backlog of orders totaling over 325,000 units in a week. This makes it clear that Toyota needs to shift its direction. Yet, since hydrogen exists infinitely in the universe and fuel cell is the ultimate energy source for generating power, Toyota should assume its role in building a new infrastructure focused on the future of a hydrogen-based society. Sakichi Toyoda once advocated an idea of "one person, one business sector" in his textile mills. Similarly, in the automotive industry, Kiichiro and Shoichiro Toyoda's divergent entry into the housing business supports the thinking habits of Akio Toyoda in the contribution to the creation and development of a pollutant-free, hydrogen-based society of the future.

There are still a large number of tasks that need to be solved as Toyota moves toward its ideal future solutions. The authors of this book wish that Toyota would maintain its practice of increasing its research toward creativeness by constantly keeping a step ahead of the times, as mentioned in the Toyoda Platform, the starting point of Toyota's thinking habit. This way it would take the seeds of innovation from its future drawers as it moves even more boldly out into the world.

PRACTICING THE PRINCIPLE OF BREAKTHROUGH THINKING TO ACTIVATE A THINKING PATH

As we have discussed up to this point, the three fundamental principles of Breakthrough Thinking as well as the four principles of Toyota's thinking habits are drastically different from traditional reductionism thinking where we seek solutions by analyzing the past and present and see them as the tools for extending into the future. The methodology of Breakthrough Thinking involves a series of steps starting with

- Focusing on humans at first
- Involving all stakeholders in redefining fundamental existential values instead of focusing on temporary or fixed solutions to meet the current needs

- Creating long-term future solutions that shift our tasks so that we do those things that drive us toward the ideal
- Implementing these new and innovative ideas with a focus on "living solutions" that change through time in accordance with the needs of the times

These require a new way of thinking along with the wisdom to survive in a world where everything is transitory on through the twenty-first century. The seventh secret ingredient to explain the reason for Toyota's strength is its practice of evolving toward an ideal future solution, and this needs to take root deep inside the organization.

TOYOTA'S GLOBAL MARKETING STRATEGY: SECRET INGREDIENT #7

A principle of the Breakthrough Thinking—Embed seeds for future innovations in your solution. There is no such thing as perpetually excellent solutions. Ask yourself every time, Did I take the next initiative?

Conventional wisdom—Why should we change something that works well now? We do not need to change it until it fails.

At Toyota—Toyota accepts as common knowledge that there is no excellent solution that works forever. Its thinking habit of seamless "daily improvement" is ingrained into Toyota. Concurrently, Toyota is promoting a philosophy of "breakthrough Toyota" that leads to a faithful practice of innovation using The Living Solution Principle, which keep changing.

Question for Reflection

Discuss why strategic marketing also calls for an ever-changing strategy.

10

The Seven Thinking Habits of Global Marketing

BYPASS THINKING IS CRITICAL

As mentioned in previous chapters, the book's author Shozo Hibino has instructed trainees coming to Japan from developing nations on how to catch fish for over 40 years. His regular training venue is near Nagoya and those trainees visit Toyota regularly. Their impression after each tour is more or less same with such comments as, "I found Toyota to be a clean place to work. It is very tidy and organized. They work like disciplined army troops." American visitors at Toyota's Kentucky plant also leave with similar comments. What is wrong with these comments? It is that those trainees were only able to comprehend Toyota by what they could see with their eyes.

Hibino has changed his approach. He now assigns the trainees to look for specific systems. Before each visit he instructs them by saying, "You are supposed to see not only the tools, like kanban or andon, but you also need to comprehend how Toyota employees have thought and acted in order to create the Toyota Production System (TPS). Think about what they needed to do over the years as they developed and implemented this system." Hibino is asking them to consider the learning process behind Toyota's thinking habit. TPS required many years of development and it is more important to learn how to catch a fish (the process that Toyota went through in the development of TPS) rather than just learning how to fish (the end result of developing the TPS). Too many experts are engaged in teaching how TPS works (fish). They only teach their students to bring that fish home for dinner (just to adopt the system). Teaching the current state of TPS will only allow potential users to catch up with Toyota, but by the time they get there, Toyota will already have progressed in leaps and bounds ahead of that point.

> The best you can ever do by copying someone else is to catch up with them. Unfortunately, by then they will also have progressed and you will still find yourself behind.

Gerhard Plenert

At this point we can see two issues. First, contrary to the Uniqueness Principle in Breakthrough Thinking and the difference of conditions between Toyota and developing countries, the experts teaching TPS are asking their students to introduce the solutions (fish) of Toyota. Those people from developing economies have not learned how to catch fish (how to create solutions) and they must forever depend on the current supply of fish (solutions) from advanced countries. This creates a dependency. The developing countries end up in the never-ending cycle of paying fees to consultants for their fish (latest and greatest solutions). Long-lasting assistance for the future should focus on a new type of assistance program enabling them to catch their own fish. It has become critical to train these countries with the thinking habits found in Breakthrough Thinking. Toyota did not simply adopt Ford Motor's conveyer system (fish). Kiichiro Toyoda comprehended the essential functions of the conveyer belt and he caught his own fish (resulting in the unique concept of just-in-time).

This phenomenon is not limited only to developing countries. In many advanced economies, we can see identical situations. Many companies are extremely eager to introduce the Toyota Production System (to eat fish) by studying it day and night. But using this process, none of them can catch up with Toyota. Toyota has already shared so many fish (solutions) but Toyota did not get a single fish (solution) from other companies. And, in spite of all of Toyota's sharing, no one has yet caught up with its performance level. By copying, they will always be behind.

What we should learn from Toyota does not come from studying the Toyota Production System (fish itself), but rather it comes from studying how Toyota thinks. It comes from understanding Toyota's process of creativity and how it acts (how to catch fish) so that we have the thinking habits tools that allow us to bypass those advanced countries and corporations.

This book was not written to tell the reader about Toyota. Rather, it is an appeal for the reader to apply and understand the importance of the thinking habits using Toyota as an exceptional case example.

MANAGEMENT USING THE SEVEN THINKING HABITS

It is important to understand that Toyota's thinking habits are compatible with Breakthrough Thinking. The reason is that Breakthrough Thinking was developed from studying the industry's high performers at both the individual and the corporate levels and understanding their thinking habits. This also requires understanding the theory that was formulated in order to support the philosophy, approach, and tools.

This book dealt with Toyota as an example and you the readers are advised to also look at those individuals and organizations around you that have demonstrated excellent performance. They are most likely using the Uniqueness Principle, thinking out in front of everyone else and setting the pace for their industry. Their stakeholders are formulating their own solutions but not by imitating anyone. They must be like Kiichiro Toyoda, who comprehended the essence of the product or process, and then incorporated a never-ending continuous improvement mindset using ultimate thinking and focused on ideal future states. They must value the interconnectedness of people and approach changes by thinking holistically, not by adopting a mechanistic approach or by applying reductionist thinking. They must also search for the essence of the process or system. They go to the actual place where the process or system is used, and by studying the actual thing they can gather relevant information allowing them to create effective solutions. And they must be able to apply creativity in order to accomplish these solutions.

Some of you may be wondering why we chase after an ideal state even if it does not work out as planned. Or you may be wondering why we discussed a Kaizen approach to change management even when it demonstrates less-than-perfect results. For those who have these concerns we recommend that you check if the seven principles have been integrated into your thinking habits. You cannot selectively pick one tool, system, or habit and assume that this one item will define success. They are integrated and need to be used in conjunction with each other. The authors would like you to find that all seven principles are functioning and interlocked. Only then can you find success. When something does not go well, there is always some aspect that has been overlooked. For instance, without defining and understanding the environment surrounding the use of a product, process, or system (the uniqueness principle), your definition of a purpose becomes too generalized and hampers your comprehension of the essence of what you are looking at. As a result, the ideal state becomes problem based and the problem usually relates back to a misunderstanding of the environment. Without ultimate thinking, you cannot get more creative, as you have nothing to focus on to try to improve. Without the involvement of those who are at the actual location of the work being done, you will end up facing their objections and backlash. By forgetting the principle of continuous improvement, your organization heads straight toward failure and bankruptcy since there will be no effective measure to take your organization to the next level, and then to the next, and so on.

The seven principles and thinking habits are interlocked. In the case of Toyota, it successfully takes these seven thinking habits and incorporates them into their internal culture. Check the current thinking habits of your company, organization, or family. When something goes wrong, there must be something missing or you are lacking the synergistic effect of all the principles working together. Once you have adopted all these principles, you will see an entirely different vision.

When we examine corporate management from the viewpoint of thinking habits, we can see large differences between a traditional, conventional management style focused on results and using the carrot-and-stick approach, as opposed to managing with Breakthrough Thinking. Toyota is a living example of the effectiveness of a business administration utilizing the seven types of thinking habits and thereby in the end bringing about impressive achievements.

TOYOTA IN PURSUIT OF "DIAMOND INNOVATION"

Toyota stands on top of the world in the automotive manufacturing sector. The reason for this achievement is attributable to its innovations and its thinking habits. Toyota has intrinsic strength within its organization, which is quite different from those companies manipulating their financial statements to show one-time-only window dressing and then later requiring bailouts. One of the primary sources of this strength can be found in the Toyota Production System.

The types of innovations can be classified as product innovation, as exemplified by the innovative development of fuel cell vehicles; process innovation, like the Toyota Production System; marketing innovation, as in the case of Toyota's U.S. market exploration; and social innovation, as shown by Toyota's social contribution toward education and pollution reduction, as well as Toyota's creation of new systems by converting its thinking so as to recognize that everything is a system in its approach for global changes. All these different kinds of innovation should be put into practice in parallel, or the innovation to transform the world will not occur. Then, when these comprehensive innovations are integrated together they are called "diamond innovations." Like a jewel, glittering from many angles, Toyota has been putting this kind of innovation methodology into practice.

In the case of the joint venture with GM in the United States, where this book's author Koichiro Noguchi took part, we find an excellent example of diamond innovation. First, the joint venture successfully triggered product innovation by moving the U.S. automotive industry into the field of compact passenger cars, which to this point had never been mainstream in the American marketplace. It also declassified what had traditionally been a Japanese-only process innovation, the Toyota Production System, and implemented it outside of Japan. This was followed by marketing innovations that explored new employment opportunities in the United States, and which in turn contributed in social innovation by organizing music events and other social activities. Finally, it used the innovation of creative thinking that led to creative innovations in the area of distribution and purchasing systems, thereby completing its diamond innovation. Toyota's global strategy began with this NUMMI (New United Motor Manufacturing Inc.) project and with this start it branched out further into the world repeatedly using the diamond innovation approach. This tells us clearly that it could not go global using only Kaizen.

This book is intended to clarify the secret sauce behind the strength of Toyota from a viewpoint of all the elements of diamond innovation utilizing Toyota's own thinking habits. Its thinking habits have been confirmed by using a new paradigm of thinking, namely, the philosophy behind Breakthrough Thinking. This approach and the theory behind it are also closely being studied academically.

Not just restricting ourselves to the case of Toyota, any individual or corporation aiming to become a top performer needs to adopt Breakthrough Thinking business management performance principles based on the seven types of thinking habits discussed in this book. Summarizing the seven thinking habits we get, "never imitate anyone, change fundamentally, pursue the ultimate and ideal state, collect the people's collective genius, see the interconnecting links and see the whole (big) picture, view everything as a system, find the essence of the system or the process,

Co-creation/believing game

1. Believe
2. +
3. X
4. Image
5. Tentative
6. Holistic
7. Unlimited
   ideas
8. No evaluation
   No debate

FIGURE 10.1
Jishu ken.

embed seeds for future innovation, and last but not least devote yourself to a hands-on approach (go and observe). As you see the effectiveness of these various practices, such as *jishu ken* where people find pleasure in studying a problem together and take advantage of the collective genius of the team (Figure 10.1), someday you will find yourself standing in the top position in your industry, as you maintain daily improvements and innovation.

Questions for Reflection

Discuss the importance of continuous improvement and of the diamond innovation approach. Describe their differences philosophically in their approach and in the tools they use.

Epilogue

THE CREEPING CRISIS FOR TOYOTA

As this book has elaborated, Toyota is currently enjoying great success with its thinking habits. With that in mind, discussing the possibility that Toyota is declining may sound alarming. It is hard to see Toyota going bankrupt at its current state. Like the proverb "Pride comes before a fall," it may someday become just another ordinary big business. It is critical for Toyota to avoid becoming a big but typical enterprise. It would be disappointing if it became a victim of the capitalism vultures on its way to bankruptcy.

By publishing and executing "The Toyota Way 2001," Toyota has been working hard to disseminate Toyota's thinking habits to its global organizations. Previously, Toyota was easily able to share its thinking habits with its relevant stakeholders because they were all close to its headquarters in Toyota city, Aichi, Japan. Being able to share its philosophy so easily then did not involve the same risk of failure as today. But today it is necessary to ask, Why should Toyota adopt "The Toyota Way 2001" now? With its rapid growth and the global expansion of its business, Toyota can no longer afford the logistics efforts of sharing its thinking habits in every new international setting, working with multinational, multiracial, and multicultural backgrounds. Moreover Toyota's thinking habits, tempered by previous generations like Ieyasu Tokugawa, the Mikawa warriors, Sakichi and Kiichiro Toyoda as well as Taiichi Ohno, have been declining as those Toyota people who were hard-invested in the original thinking habits are retiring. This book is focused on the thinking habits that have defined the uniqueness of Toyota. But there is a growing chance that the unique thinking habits that have made Toyota what it is may disappear. This has Toyota's top management officers worried. This concern was originally behind the creation of "The Toyota Way 2001." However, Toyota's fate depends on how seriously it finds value in succeeding to pass along its thinking habits. When Toyota's thinking habits weaken, it may eventually turn the company into just another ordinary big business full of internal power struggles, similar to what happened to the Sharp Corporation.

We see the creation of a Toyota crisis situation. The risk already appears to be around the corner, and we who are involved with Toyota are afraid.

HOW TOYOTA SHOULD AVOID ITS RISK

For Toyota the best strategic options are

1. To innovate continuously—In order to succeed Toyota needs to continue to deliberately and strenuously develop Toyota's thinking habits. Its thinking habits were cultivated for over 500 years since Ieyasu Tokugawa and incorporated in the Toyoda methodology. This is a source of Toyota's vitality. It is critical for them to prevent its decay into just an ordinary big enterprise, bouncing with the ups and downs of markets, and employing popularly accepted general principles found in case studies.

    Henry Ford, aka the automotive king, said, "If there is a secret to success in everything, it should be none other than a talent to comprehend the views of others and see things from another's standpoint other than his own." The biggest feature of this book has been in clearly defining the latent conventional thinking habits of Toyota from the unique standpoint of Breakthrough Thinking as well as clarifying that this could be integrated as the organization's seven thinking habits. The authors of this book sincerely hope that its readers succeed in incorporating the excellent thinking habits defined in this book and use them to achieve success.

2. To achieve 100% customer satisfaction—As advocated by Kiichiro Toyoda, this is the essence of Toyota's global marketing strategy. In order to take the approach of thinking from the viewpoint of the customer in its demand chain requires building and running the business so that it will satisfy all stakeholders at each stage of the demand chain including designing with the design-in approach, production, scrapping, recycling, and so on. This requires giving everyone a positive benefit where everyone wins using Breakthrough Thinking.

3. To pursue the diamond innovation approach as the leader of a seamless improvement and innovation methodology—Toyota should leap ahead in such new technologies as artificial intelligence, the Internet of things, and autonomous drive. Toyota should

drive toward creativity in research and innovation, and always stay ahead of the times as written in the Toyoda Platform. This would lead an organization to becoming a diamond innovation enterprise, showing excellence in every dimension.

4. To avoid internal power struggles as seen in far too many companies today—Toyota needs to sustain strong corporate unity, as the Mikawa warriors used to do. This requires determination, holding fast to another principle of the Toyoda Platform, which is to display the spirit of fraternity and to encourage a family-like culture.

Practicing all the above would help Toyota to avoid a potential crisis. In conclusion, let us again refer to the words of former Toyota president Shoichiro Toyoda: "I have depended on the following five practices in my own management:

- *Genchi-Genbutsu* (observe the actual things at actual places—sometimes referred to as the Gemba walk),
- Quality should be built into the process,
- Price is determined in the marketplace,
- Challenge everything in order to achieve seamless innovations, and
- Improve your human resources."

Appendix: Global Network of Toyota

Global Production Sites

Country/Region	Company Name[a]	Production Since	Major Product	Toyota Vehicle Output ('Thousand Units)[b]
North America				
Canada	1. Canadian Autoparts Toyota Inc. (CAPTIN)	1985	Aluminum wheels	–
	2. Toyota Motor Manufacturing Canada Inc. (TMMC)	1988	Corolla, Matrix, RX350, RAV 4	579
United States	3. TABC, Inc.	1972	Catalyzer, steering column: metal Stamping	–
	4. Toyota Motor Manufacturing, Kentucky, Inc. (TMMK)	1988	Camry, Camry Hybrid, Avalon, Venza	466
			Engine	–
	5. Bodine Aluminum, Inc.	1993	Aluminum casting	–
	6. Toyota Motor Manufacturing, West Virginia, Inc. (TMMWV)	1998	Engine, transmission	–
	7. Toyota Motor Manufacturing, Indiana, Inc. (TMMI)	1999	Sequoia, Highlander, Sienna	350
	8. Toyota Motor Manufacturing, Alabama, Inc. (TMMAL)	2003	Engine	–
	9. Toyota Motor Manufacturing, Texas, Inc. (TMMTX)	2006	Tundra, Tacoma	237
	10. Subaru of Indiana Automotive, Inc. (SIA)	2007 (consignment)	Camry	93

(*Continued*)

Country/Region	Company Name[a]	Production Since	Major Product	Toyota Vehicle Output (Thousand Units)[b]
	11. Toyota Motor Manufacturing, Mississippi, Inc. (TMMMS)	2011	Corolla	189
Latin America				
Argentina	12. Toyota Argentina S.A. (TASA)	1997	Hilux, Fortuner	96
Brazil	13. Toyota do Brasil Ltda. (TDB)	1959	Corolla, Etios	162
Mexico	14. Toyota Motor Manufacturing de Baja California, S. de R.L. de C.V. (TMMBC)	2004	Tacoma	71
Venezuela	15. Toyota de Venezuela Compania Anonima (TDV)	1981	Lekki Corolla, Fortuner, Hilux	– 3
Europe				
Czech Republic	16. Toyota Peugeot Citroën Automobiles Czech, s.r.o. (TPCA)	2005	Aygo	203
France	17. Toyota Motor Manufacturing France S.A.S. (TMMF)	2001	Yaris	225
Poland	18. Toyota Motor Manufacturing Poland SP.zo.o. (TMMP)	2002	Engine, transmission	–
	19. Toyota Motor Industries Poland SP.zo.o. (TMIP)	2005	Engine	–
Portugal	20. Toyota Caetano Portugal, S.A. (TCAP)	1968	Dyna	2

(Continued)

Country/Region	Company Name[a]	Production Since	Major Product	Toyota Vehicle Output ('Thousand Units)[b]
Turkey	21. Toyota Motor Manufacturing Turkey Inc. (TMMT)	1994	Verso, Corolla	130
UK	22. Toyota Motor Manufacturing (UK) Ltd. (TMUK)	1992	Avensis, Auris, Auris Hybrid	171
			Engine	–
Russia	23. Limited Liability Company "Toyota Motor Manufacturing Russia" (TMMR)	2007	Camry	36
	24. OOO Sollers-Bussan	2013	Land Cruiser	14
Kazakhstan	53. Saryarka AvtoProm LLP (SAP)	2014	Fortuner	–
Africa				
Kenya	25. Associated Vehicle Assemblers Ltd. (AVA)	1977	Land Cruiser	1
Republic of South Africa	26. Toyota South Africa Motors (Pty) Ltd. (TSAM)	1962	Corolla, Fortuner, Hilux, Dyna	149
Egypt	27. Arab American vehicle Co. (AAV)	2012 (consignment)	Fortuner	–
Asia				
China	28. Tianjin Fengjin Automobile Transmission Parts Co., Ltd. (TFAP)	1998	Axel, CVJ	–

(Continued)

Country/Region	Company Name[a]	Production Since	Major Product	Toyota Vehicle Output (Thousand Units)[b]
	29. Tianjin FAW Toyota Engine Co., Ltd. (TFTE)	1998	Engine	–
	30. Tianjin Toyota Forging Parts Co., Ltd. (TTFC)	1998	Forging, CVJ	–
	31. Tianjin FAW Toyota Motor Co., Ltd. (TFTM)	2002	Vios, Corolla, Crown, Reiz, RAV4	442
	32. FAW-Toyota Changchun Engine Co., Ltd. (FTCE)	2004	Engine	–
	33. Guangqi Toyota Co., Ltd. (GTE)	2005	Engine	–
	34. Sichuan FAW Toyota Co., Ltd. (SFTM)	1999	Coaster, Land Cruiser, Land Cruiser Prado, Prius	145
	35. Guangqi Toyota Co., Ltd. (GTMC)	2006	Camry, Yaris, Highlander, Camry Hybrid	380
	54. Toyota Motor (Changshu) Auto Parts Co., Ltd. (TMCAP)	2014	Transmission	–
Taiwan	36. Kuozui Motors, Ltd.	1986	Camry, Corolla, Wish, Vios, Yaris, Innova	200
			Engine; Metal Stamping	–
India	37. Toyota Kirloskar Motor Private Ltd. (TKM)	1999	Corolla, Innova, Fortuner, Etios	148
	38. Toyota Kirloskar Auto Parts Private Ltd. (TKAP)	2002	Axel, propeller shaft, transmission	–

(Continued)

Country/Region	Company Name[a]	Production Since	Major Product	Toyota Vehicle Output ('Thousand Units)[b]
Indonesia	39. PT. Toyota Motor Manufacturing Indonesia (TMMIN)	1970	Innova, Fortuner, Avanza	209
			Engine	–
	40. PT. Astra Daihatsu Motor (ADM)	2003 (consignment)	Avanza	199
	41. PT. Hino Motors Manufacturing Indonesia (HMMI)	2009 (consignment)	Dyna	12
	42. PT. Sugity Creatives		Noah	–
Malaysia	43. Assembly Services Sdn. Bhd. (ASSB)	1968	Hiace, Vios, Hilux, Innova, Fortuner	80
			Engine	–
Pakistan	44. Indus Motor Company Ltd. (IMC)	1993	Corolla, Hilux	42
Philippines	45. Toyota Motor Philippines Corp. (TMP)	1989	Innova, Vios	42
	46. Toyota Autoparts Philippines Inc. (TAP)	1992	Transmission, constant velocity joint	–
Thailand	47. Toyota Motor Thailand Co, Ltd. (TMT)	1964	Corolla, Camry, Camry Hybrid, Prius, Vios, Yaris, Hilux, Fortuner	725
	48. Siam Toyota Manufacturing Co, Ltd. (STM)	1989	Engine, propeller shaft	–
	49. Toyota Auto Works Co, Ltd. (TAW)		Hiace	7

(Continued)

Country/Region	Company Name[a]	Production Since	Major Product	Toyota Vehicle Output ('Thousand Units)[b]
Vietnam	50. Toyota Motor Vietnam Co., Ltd. (TMV)	1996	Camry, Corolla, Vios, Innova, Hiace, Fortuner	35
Oceania				
Australia	51. Toyota Motor Corporation Australia Ltd. (TMCA)	1963	Camry, Camry Hybrid	90
			Engine	–
Middle East				
Bangladesh	52. Aftab Automobiles Ltd.	1982	Land Cruiser	–

Source: Toyota Global Newsroom.

Note: All data as of the end of December 2014.

[a] Numbers before company name correspond to the map in Chapter 3, Figure 3.3.

[b] Toyota vehicle output, excluding knockdown (KD) and original equipment manufacturer (OEM), are listed for over 1000 units.

Regional Supervising Corporations

Country	Company Name	Established	Major Function
United States	Toyota Motor North America, Inc. (TMA)	1996	Public relations, publicity and research for the whole of North America
	Toyota Motor Engineering & Manufacturing North America, Inc. (TEMA)	2006	Research and development in North America; coordination of production in North America
	Toyota Motor Sales, U.S.A., Inc. (TMS)	1957	Coordination of sales in North America
Belgium	Toyota Motor Europe NV/SA (TME)	2005	Coordination of Toyota operations in Europe
Singapore	Toyota Motor Asia Pacific Pte Ltd. (TMAP-MS)	1990	Parts supply to ASEAN (Association of Southeast Asian Nations); support of marketing and sales in Asia
Thailand	Toyota Motor Asia Pacific Engineering and Manufacturing Co., Ltd. (TMAP-EM)	2003	Support local production in Asia/Oceania/Middle East by development and evaluation
China	Toyota Motor (China) Investment Co., Ltd. (TMCI)	2001	Public relation and publicity in China; sales of imports including Lexus

Bibliography

Henry Ford, *20seiki no kyojin jitsugyoka; Henry Ford no kiseki* [Giant entrepreneurs of the 20th century: Henry Ford's trajectory], Sanseido, 2012.

Shozo Hibino, *Papa Mama Sozo Riron* [Papa and mama creation theory], Kodansha, 2004.

Shozo Hibino, *Toppa no Kagaku* [Science of breaking-through], Editaashippu, 2003.

Shozo Hibino, *Toyota No Shikoshukan* [Toyota's thinking habit], Kodansha, 2005.

Hajime Hibino and Shozo Hibino, *Bureikusuruu Shiko No Susume* [A guide to Breakthrough Thinking], Maruzen, 2004.

Ayaka Himoto and Shozo Hibino (supervisor), *Bureikusuruu Tore-ningu* [Workbook of Breakthrough Thinking], Nihon Jitsugyo Shuppan-sha, 2016.

Ayaka Himoto and Shozo Hibino (supervisor), *Kikakuno Tatsujin* [Master of planning], Soubi C.C. Labo, 2004.

Satoshi Iwanaka, *Shussinken de wakaru Hitono seikaku* [Personality identified from what prefecture he comes from], Soshi-sha, 2003.

H.T. Johnson et al. *Toyota wa naze tsuyoika* [Profit beyond measure], Nihon Keizai Shimbun-sha.

Kazuaki Kajiwara, *Toyota Wuei* [Toyota Way], Bijinesu-sha, 2002.

Hiromu Kajiwara and Shozo Hibino, *Bureikusuruu* [Breakthrough], Kodansha.

Hideharu Kaneda, *Toyota-shiki saikyō no keiei : naze Toyota wa kawaritsuzukeru no ka*, Nihon Keizai Shimbun-sha.

Jeffrey K. Liker, *Za Toyota Wuei* [The Toyota Way], Nikkei BP, 2003.

Gerald Nadler and Shozo Hibino, *Breakthrough Thinking*, Prima, 1990.

Gerald Nadler and Shozo Hibino, *Bureikusuruu Shiko* [Breakthrough thinking], Daiyamonndo-sha, 1991.

Gerald Nadler and Shozo Hibino, *Creative Solution Finding*, Prima, 1994.

Gerhard Plenert and Shozo Hibino, *Making Innovation Happen*, St. Lucie Press, 1997.

Shaapu houkai [Sharp collapsed], Nihon Keizai Shimbun Shuppan-sha. Others resources include articles in the Nihon Keizai Shimbun and television news, 2016.

Masaaki Satoh, *Za Hausu obu Toyota* [The House of Toyota], Bungei Shunjuu, 2009.

Ryotaro Shiba, *Haoo no iye* [House of Supreme Ruler] Shincho Publishing Inc., 2002.

Ryotaro Shiba, *Rekishi wo tabisuru* [Walking along with history], Shincho-sha, 2010.

Nihon Keizai Shimbun, *Shaapu houkai* [Sharp collapsed], Nihon Keizai Shimbun Shuppan-sha.

Hironori Shiramizu, "Kakushin wo michibiku manejimennto" [Management to incite innovations], *JMA Management Review*, vol. 10, no. 12, pp. 9–12, Nihon Norritsu Kyokai (JMA).

Toshiyuki Takagi, *Toyota Saikyo Kigyo no Tetsugaku* [Philosophy of Toyota, the strongest], Jitsugyo no Nihon-sha, 2003.

Eiji Toyoda, *Ketsudan* [Determination], Nikkei Bijinesu Bunko, 2000.

Shoichiro Toyoda, *Mirai wo shinji ippo zutsu* [Step by step, believing in the future], Nihon Keizai Shimbun Shuppan-sha, 2015.

Kiyoshi Tsukamoto, *Saikyo Toyota no DNA Kakumei* [DNA revolution of Toyota, the strongest], Kodan-sha, 2002.

Yoshihito Wakamatsu, *Toyota-ryu Shigotono Tetsugaku* [Toyota style job philosophy], PHP, 2013.

WEDGE, [The day of Auto Industry Disappearing] vol. 17, no. 6, Wedge Inc.

Index